*DNA is a large part* [...]
*what you become: I dedicate this book to*
*my entrepreneurial grandfather, whom I looked*
*up to, and who inspired me.*

# Contents

# Introduction

Innovation, the key to your company's survival, must be encoded in your corporate DNA. It is an *imperative*—because you can bet your competitors are going at innovation full-bore.

This is true regardless of the size of your organization, no matter what business you're in or what product or service you provide. More so today than ever before, innovation is the holistic strategy that savvy leaders create, that flourishes in the right atmosphere (and founders in the wrong environment). Cultivated properly, with teams empowered and impassioned to do their best, innovation is the surefire way to development of marketplace showstoppers that build value for organization stakeholders.

Innovation takes guts. It's not for the faint of heart and the weak of will. I refer to a famous quote from U.S. President Theodore Roosevelt at the Sorbonne in Paris, back in 1910. In his speech, entitled "The Man in the Arena," our former Rough Rider President said:

> It is not the critic who counts: not the man who points out how the strong man stumbles, or where the doer of deeds could have done them better. The

credit belongs to the man who is actually in the arena, whose face is marred by dust and sweat and blood; who strives valiantly; who errs, who comes short again and again, because there is no effort without error and shortcoming; but who does actually strive to do the deeds; who knows great enthusiasms, the great devotions; who spends himself in a worthy cause; who at the best knows in the end the triumph of high achievement, and who at the worst, if he fails, at least fails while daring greatly, so that his place shall never be with those cold and timid souls who neither know victory nor defeat.

My name is Robert Brands. I was born and raised in the Netherlands, and, over the years, I have led companies around the world, and have managed, teamed with, mentored, and learned from an impressive group of dynamic, creative leaders. Some are fellow Vistage members (www.vistage.com) such as Jeff DeFazio and Jaynie Smith, one of this C-level organization's most sought-after speakers and author of *Creating Competitive Advantage*. "A company must create competitive advantages if they are not to rely on price as their differentiator," she says. "The road to significant competitive advantages depends on a culture of innovation."

We come from different cultures, grew up speaking different languages, and prospered in very different industries. But there are important traits we have in common.

- *We are not afraid to fail.* We know how to break down the barriers that derail innovation. How to encourage creativity that leads to breakthrough products

and service. How to introduce systems and procedures that outmaneuver the competition now and in
years to come.

- *We know people are resistant to change.* And, importantly, we have the will to win the doubters over
and build value for our organizations—often in the
face of firmly entrenched corporate cultures and
silo-driven territorial behavior patterns.

- *We are, in a very real sense, a fraternity of like-
minded professionals.* We are passionate about the
importance of innovation for the long term—
sustainable innovation, if you will. And it's heart-
ening to find that professionals with this mind-set are
truly found all over the world.

And that is good news for you. I have captured in these
pages decades worth of my collective, invaluable experience. I call them Robert's Rules of Innovation, and much
like the *Robert's Rules of Order,* which create order from
chaos in meetings around the world, they will help you
understand the principles needed to create, nurture,
profit from, and sustain a solid new product development
(NPD) program.

The bookstores and online sellers offer stacks of comprehensive, detailed texts on innovation, and on various
approaches to generating innovation. My challenge, as I
continued my work with companies the world over, was to
create a hands-on, understandable, practical approach that
readers can use easily and benefit from quickly, as in *today.*
And I literally mean right this very minute. Because, let's
face it, whether you manage a multinational or an entrepreneurial start-up, whether you are a not-for-profit, manufacturer, distributor, service provider, supplier, or retailer,

the pressures today—in terms of time, budget, *everything*—are unprecedented in our lifetimes.

So let me introduce you to the best thinking of my international network of innovators. Together, we will show you how to start, nurture, and profit from a culture of sustained innovation in the work environment. We share our experiences in "sidebar" case histories throughout the book, and to help you focus on next steps for your organization, every chapter concludes with "Think About" points we hope you'll find valuable.

Passionate about creativity? Ready to unleash your team's abilities? Eager to create the next home-run new product?

Welcome, then, to *Robert's Rules of Innovation*.

# 1

# Innovation, Survival, and the "Aha!" Moment

Remember back in the dark ages of, oh, several years ago, where in some quarters it was legitimate to actually ask questions like:

- Should we innovate?
- Should we create a new product development (NPD) program?
- How necessary is our research-and-development (R&D) department, anyway?

That last one in particular makes me cringe. All of these questions, though, seem quaint in the context of today's business environment. It's war out there. You innovate. *Period.* If you don't innovate, you perish (Exhibit 1.1). Simple as that. If you are reading this book, you know that failure simply is not an option.

With innovation no longer a choice, the next question for many of the thousands of otherwise thoughtful

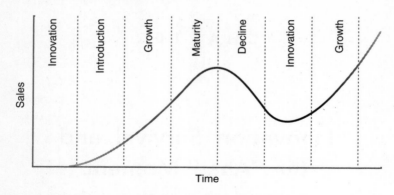

**Exhibit 1.1     Innovation Restarts the Product Life Cycle**

executives I've met over the years—in a wide variety of industries—is, "Okay, we need to innovate. But how?" or, "Okay, but we already have an NPD program in place, but it's not working. You're consistently late to market."

Where do you start? How do you fashion a program that works within the context of your organization and its unique culture?

You've come to the right place. If you've read this far, you know that innovation is the lifeblood of new business. You want to outperform the competition but are unsure of how to proceed. Maybe you've benefited from an innovative product or service but have been unable to recreate this past success with any degree of regularity. Or perhaps you face a mandate to cut budgets to the bone—the so-called addition by subtraction. One of the first budget line items to be cut is often R&D—the very *last* thing that should be eliminated during uncertain times.

In today's business environment, *Robert's Rules of Innovation* will help you create order from the chaos—clearly, concisely, and helpfully. The cornerstone of *Robert's Rules of Innovation* is the set of 10 essential rules of innovation implementation to create and sustain *new* business, detailed in Chapter 2. These rules are distilled from my decades of experience as a leader of international product development teams, as well as input from my international network of professional sources with experience on a wide variety of products and services.

## How Do I Get to "Aha!"?

Throughout my professional career, my orientation has been spent on new product introductions. While at Philips Lighting as Manager–New Products, I developed the first version of an NPD stage-gate process and refined this process in roles and companies that followed, such as GTE Sylvania and Kohler.

One highlight of my career came at a company I headed, called Airspray. Take a look in your kitchen, bath, or cupboard—in the United States, in Europe, in the Pacific Rim. See those instant-foam dispensers, most likely hand soaps—the ones that work without chemicals or propellants? Dishwashing liquids? Cleansers? We pioneered that dispensing technology and created a ubiquitous presence in every household, in both developed and emerging markets. (See Exhibit 1.2.)

I am often asked how we did it. How did we get to that *"Aha!"* moment, when we knew we had a dispensing design that would turn the personal care product industry on its head? Once the technology was perfected, how did we sell it in one market segment after another? How did we protect our investment and ward off industry newcomers? How did we build a worldwide team and overcome the

**Exhibit 1.2    Foaming Hand Soap**
*Source:* Rexam Airspray, B.V.

cultural differences inherent in a multinational effort? And how did we build upon our first designs to keep trade customer, retailer, and consumer interest (and profitability) high?

The answer: **innovation**. It's an overused word and very broad in meaning. Before we continue, let's take a closer look at what I mean when I use the word *innovation*.

One of my professional associates, a true product innovator, Peter Dircks, is the Vice President of Product Management and New Product Development at Hearth & Home Technologies. According to Peter, who has just redesigned his company's flagship product line, true innovation is the optimum balance achieved by using the latest technologies, cost structures, styling, features, and services, and then successfully delivering that which is "new" to match customer or end-user needs at the optimum price.

"One needs to look only at the iPod as a perfect example," he says. "End users wanted the ability to purchase single songs, versus entire albums, as well as to easily categorize and organize their MP3s and have all the information from the music industry. Apple delivered on this by leveraging the use of the Internet (technology), developing highly intuitive software (iTunes), as well as utilizing their music industry contracts (distribution and royalty agreements) with a very cool physical product (the iPod itself, its styling, user interface, etc.)."

According to Peter, "this is one of the best examples of true innovation, in my opinion, and why they have such a global market share MP3 player lead in what could have been a commodity product, like the TV."

Great example, Peter, yet let's bear in mind that while innovation used to relate primarily with manufactured "things" (products), companies have recently innovated new services as well, as evidenced by new offerings in banking, real estate, and insurance—the reverse mortgage comes quickly to mind.

And there are hybrids as well: new products accompanied by an innovative service. Again, the iPod model—super electronics bundled with iTunes accounts for managing downloads and personal music libraries.

Here is yet another take on how to think about innovation, from my friend Bruce Sauter, who studied industrial design and was a driving force at Atari and, later, at a division of Kohler Company. His incredible mind sits comfortably at the confluence of product design, aesthetics, and the product's emotional tie to the end user.

"As I progressed in my career, my roles expanded to give insight into the fact that, for innovation to work and be sustainable, it must be the DNA of the organization—one with visionary leadership," Bruce told me. "Innovation is a holistic strategy for building organizational culture, empowering the passion to create, developing creative environments that can execute effectively, and creating the potential for market leadership."

"Innovation," he continued, "is not just happening in the front end of the business development process—it needs to be pervasive throughout the entire value chain."

According to Bruce, and I think you'll agree, innovation appeals to those of us who are passionate about creativity, working in dynamic teams through hard times and good times, building upon the free exchange of ideas and the successful execution of those concepts that results in a win. When an idea is discovered and implemented across the value chain with success, a "sweet spot" is hit—right on the mark. It's like winning the big game together.

Innovation is a cumulative process. It takes time and lots of energy. It is seeing people grow, open up, and succeed. This is one of the great by-products of innovation, he said. Successful organizations have successful people.

What it all boils down to is this: finding, empowering, and fostering individuals and teams with the passion to create their environments where they do their work, and play, and continually improve efforts to sustain the outcome. The rush you feel when things come together in just the right way and result in market leadership—that's what it's all about for me.

Successful innovators will tell you over and over again, and it's important to reflect on it here as well: Innovation is not just about "creating new stuff." It's about creating an organizational process that encourages the creation of new methods, ideas, and, yes, products. It's all about instituting a different way of thinking, doing, and creating value.

With all this innovation taking place—from new widgets to new insurance products to new processes—it has become more important than ever for business leaders to institute innovation programs and *manage* them effectively.

Usually, I avoid clichés (like the plague!). But the cliché has its purpose: It is based on a common experience, a real issue faced all the time. And the cliché that comes to mind here, regarding innovation, is this:

> *Fail fast, but fail cheap.*

In the dark ages, NPD program participants ideated and created a new product and passed the torch to sales and marketing. Today, however, there are more complex issues within the organization that require flexible structures and unprecedented cooperation across disciplines, teams, and business units.

So we now need bold tools such as new organizational structures, new forms of training, procedures, intracompany communications, and bold leaders who understand and can implement consensus across divisional and geographic boundaries.

## Innovation Is Not a Luxury

At this point, I know what some of you may be thinking:

> We're a smaller company, with less than $50 million in annual revenue. We don't have the time,

manpower, or money for this type of comprehensive innovation initiative. Why can't we just "wing it" like we usually do?

As this is written, the media's stream of negative financial news appears infinite. Earnings are off. Consumer spending is down. Savings rates are up (maybe that's not such a bad thing, though). Layoffs. Deleveraging. 401(k)s that are now "201(k)s."

"How can we afford an innovation program?" you ask. "Maybe when things get better, we can revisit innovation," others might say. Like putting off that European vacation, postponing the purchase of that new Beemer, shelving the kitchen remodeling. Luxuries can be delayed, right?

Remember, innovation is not a luxury, even for today's most successful companies. Sustaining success means ongoing renewal of your intellectual property (IP) portfolio. After all, technologies become dated; end-user fashions change; and new processes, materials, and capabilities emerge. Like breakers at the seashore, the life cycle of a technology begins, crests, and falls off as, all the while, new technologies form and carry momentum of their own—an ongoing cycle of innovation energy, if you will. Exhibit 1.3 will help you visualize the "waves" of technology.

At Airspray, we applied this philosophy but extended sales growth from the initial hair care product to skin care, to hand soap, to foaming body wash.

Innovation is a must-have. It's your company's lifeblood. And remember, too, the perfect time to ramp up your innovation efforts is exactly when your cash-strapped competitors are slashing their programs. Especially if you believe that we are in a major, global economic shift, not just a garden-variety, cyclical downturn.

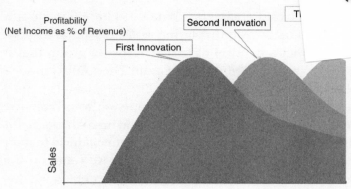

Exhibit 1.3  **Repeating Innovation Is Critical to Sustaining Above-Average Long-Term Profits**
*Source:* Brands & Company, LLC.

*BusinessWeek* magazine recently reported on this very issue. "Innovation is an easy target," says Vijay Govindarajan, a professor at Dartmouth's Tuck School of Business. "R&D dollars, by definition, lead to uncertain outcomes. Companies don't want failures during difficult times."[*]

Some companies are taking an innovation vacation, resting on past successes, making incremental changes to successful products. But others, the smart ones, are looking at ways to reposition existing technologies in order to appeal to new end-user audiences. Here's an example: Guitar Hero. The technology itself is cool, but not earth-shattering. What's innovative is that its makers have captured the imagination of customers who had not been

---

[*]Reena Jana, "Is Innovation Too Costly in Hard Times?" *BusinessWeek,* April 9, 2009.

considered typical "gamers." When you have 55-year-olds rocking out to Aerosmith, playing with a toy guitar without knowing even a handful of basic chords—a group that is not typically associated with the Grand Theft Auto crowd—you've done something creative.

Redirecting customer appeal is one way to be creative. Of course, there is also the technological breakthrough, for example, the aforementioned Airspray mechanical foamer in the world of hand soaps. At the time we came on the scene, the key innovations in hand soaps were:

*Early 20th century:* The invention of the bar soap available at retail.

*1970s:* The launch of liquid soaps.

Nothing had changed in hand soap packaging for decades, and the market was primed for something new. Along we came, with a dispensing solution that offered real consumer benefits in a final "medium" that consumers really wanted—foam (Dripless! Easy to use! More efficient cleaning! Kid friendly! Fun!)—and offered true product differentiation at the point of sale.

Then there is innovation through change in the business model—how can your company wring incremental revenues out of the current value chain? Again, this method is exemplified by Apple and its iPod. It's more than a device. It's more than a service. It's a lifestyle must-have that has become embedded in our daily lives.

There are three themes for innovation, and all address the ultimate goal: to create value in the minds of your customers, whether you sell business to business or directly to end users/consumers. Innovation is not a luxury to be placed on the back burner. Innovation builds brands, which means profitable growth, which means marketplace success.

## Where Does Innovation Begin?

There are plenty of reasons to innovate, especially in times such as these. Yet the question still begs: What are the key issues around getting started?

- How do you set the policy?
- How do you build a quality team and an environment that fosters teamwork?
- Is it really possible to work with your customers and keep them involved in the process?
- How can you make the organizational changes needed to facilitate your efforts?
- What's the best way to harness marketing to encourage marketplace demand for, and acceptance of, the innovations to come—prime the pump, so to speak?

These topics will come up again in greater detail later on in this book, but for now I've asked my friend and associate Jill McCurdy to weigh in. Jill is an ideation expert and runs the Innovation Center for Rexam's Plastics Division. She addresses a key concern about innovation programs: how to maximize their performance (i.e., how to enhance the financial return on their investment in innovation).

A key factor, Jill explains, is turbo-charging the ideation process, through creating the right kind of processes, being the right kind of leader, and selecting the right team. Her insights are valuable to a wide range of executives, in companies large and small.

"When I think of ideation that goes awry, I think of too much overplanning," she said. "Way too much." By that, she means too much emphasis on cutesy rooms, with lots of props and scenarios purchased in the hope of spurring the ideation team to dizzying heights of creativity.

"It's great to start with some creative play to get the ball rolling. You want to set the stage with visual tools, but just enough. In my experience, it's more about real strategies, and problem solving, and harnessing the right people," she said.

Paramount is starting with a specific problem in mind, which helps focus, or channel, the energy in the room and create just the right environment for success. Innovation objectives must correlate with business objectives, and these must be effectively communicated to the team.

Another key: building a knowledgeable group attuned to customer or end-user needs. And the group should be diverse, from across functions, divisions, age groups, gender lines, ethnic backgrounds, and company levels. A diverse group, she explained, creates the tension and interplay that can take the team to new, unexpected places.

How diverse is *diverse*? Actually, some innovation experts encourage inclusion of customers in the core group, to simultaneously help generate ideas through widened perspectives and build relationships in the process. Working in partnership with customers can also help accelerate time to market and lead to custom solutions that result in enhanced capabilities and expertise, Jill said. Risky? Perhaps so. And, in fact, we'll later hear from an expert who is strongly against mixing your team's creative folks with the client or customer.

But the potential payoff for daring collaborations is the creation of high(er)-margin products, hence improved return on investment (ROI) on your innovation program.

As for structuring the process, clearly this varies widely and is dependent on the size of the organization. The nimble, smaller, more entrepreneurial company may have its NPD team run by the chief executive officer, with a core group of three or four other team players. The process is often a bit less formal, and there are fewer projects to track.

But smaller companies can have a great deal at risk, and innovation can loom as a do-or-die imperative. Therefore, processes are in place to ensure proper tracking from ideation to finished product.

According to Jill, the innovation process is clearly a left brain/right brain exercise. "You need the strategy piece, structure, and logic—as well as the intuitive, more random thinking processes," she said. Once upon a time, structure in ideation was considered antithetical to creativity, but no more. "It's all about the balance between planning, ideation, and analysis of the session—and the actual doing," she said. "Neither should stifle the other, and it's up to the leader of the team to make sure the group is on the right track."

*Up to the leader of the team.* What are the personality characteristics of the ideal leader? What is the skill set? Clearly, the leader of the innovation team is a make-or-break factor in the group's success. It is important to recognize that the characteristics of the successful entrepreneur often do not overlap with the characteristics of the innovation team leader. It's important for the team leader to be able to "give stage" to others in the group, to be a good listener and capable of patiently facilitating sessions composed of the aforementioned diverse groups.

The team leader has to have the gift of personality and managerial skills that allows team members to think the right way. He or she has to be the cheerleader for the initiative, the keeper of the culture, which includes excitement and recognition of success. The leader needs to involve all members of the team and balance the emotional needs of both the team's alpha dogs and its more reticent members. In a nutshell, the leader champions the entire innovation enterprise.

Based on my experience in a wide range of midsized and smaller firms, sometimes the "little guys" (the smaller firms) have an edge in terms of creating and sustaining the culture of innovation. Innovation may be more of an imperative than in larger, process-driven companies. And, even more to the point, in the smaller outfits, interaction between engineers, sales, marketing, production, and C-level executives is more regular and comfortable. Listening to each other is more of an ongoing occurrence.

Above all, innovation leadership must instill and monitor the process discipline that leads to a positive, innovation-driven, ROI story. This includes scheduling regular meetings, setting financial guidelines, establishing timelines and goals for NPD programs, and assigning responsibilities.

The successful innovation leader cares about more than determining the optimal time of day to hold the ideation meetings (although regularly scheduled meetings are important, and we'll learn why later in this book). He or she is about more than incentives, using creative exercises to get the synapses popping, encouraging the participation of quieter group members and tempering the enthusiasm of the alphas.

The successful innovator builds the culture brick by brick, top down, and reinforces it—every day, in every way—and can dynamically, persuasively, intelligently, and passionately challenge the team to new levels of success for mutual benefit, turning great ideas into showstopper products and services that lead to incremental sales.

Ready to begin? Then read on for the Innovator's Manifesto.

## Think About

- How would you describe the tone and outcome of your most recent ideation sessions?
- What was the result of your last ideation/partnership with a customer?
- In terms of group diversity, are there others who might contribute to the team?
- What recent marketplace innovation do you admire?
- What recent innovation from *your* company are you proudest of?

# CHAPTER 2

# The Innovator's Manifesto
## ROBERT'S RULES OF INNOVATION

You're wide awake, in bed, and your spouse and kids are sound asleep. Down the hall, your dog snores blissfully. You peek at the alarm clock and drop your head back down to your pillow. It's 3:37 A.M.

What's keeping you up at night? If you're like me and the people I know, it's concern over your business. The competition is relentless. Customers are restless, sharpening their pencils with every order. Consumers are antsy, spending less of their dwindling disposable income, thanks in part to the steady drumbeat of negative reports from our 24/7 news cycle.

Is it any wonder you're awake again in the middle of the night? It's chaos out there, isn't it?

It's time to make order from the chaos, like H. M. Robert did, back in 1876, when he created *Robert's Rules of Order*—the iconic rules and imperatives that turn gatherings from Towers of Babel into well-run, smoothly functioning meetings, sheer models of decorum and, more importantly, productivity.

**Robert's Rules of Innovation** gives you 10 steps to create and sustain "new" in Business, delivering profitable growth through **i-n-n-o-v-a-t-i-o-n**, from the "I" of *Inspiration*, to the "N" of *Net Results*. Here, I address all the parameters needed for a successful, lasting innovation strategy and execution.

Bear in mind, these are "rules of order"—for innovation requires rules of the house, rules that must be implemented, maintained, protected, and fostered—fiercely—in order for your innovation program to succeed. Innovation is the lifeblood of any company, and Robert's Rules of Innovation is the heart of your sustainable growth strategy.

 **I**nspire

 **N**o Risk, No Innovation

 **N**ew Product Development Process

 **O**wnership

 **V**alue Creation

 **A**ccountability

 **T**raining and Coaching

 **I**dea Management

 **O**bserve and Measure

 **N**et Result and Reward

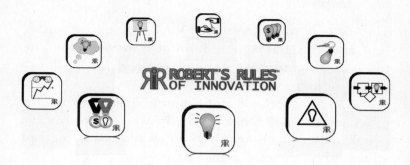

Let's now take a look at each of the rules, and understand why each is so critical to the creation of sustained innovation.

**Inspire**

The leader of your innovation SWAT team has to inspire, lead, and drive the process. Buy-in has to come from the top; it has to be an integral part of your company's culture. This is an imperative.

It can't be a "flavor of the month" effort. Short-term programs are sniffed out quickly by your company's key people, with deleterious effects. Remember back in grade school, when the class would arrive in the morning and find a substitute teacher in front of the classroom? Do you remember what happened on such days? Mayhem.

For the innovation program to work, the leader—and in many smaller and midsized companies, that person is the chief executive officer (CEO)—has to be regularly and personally involved, so that everyone understands, "This is the way it's going to be. This is what I expect. There are no exceptions. We are all in this together. We will make it work. And we will all reap the rewards of this program."

And the unspoken implication: *or else.*

A major tip on setting the culture, so that it is an unassailable, undeniable, inescapable part of life at your company: Set regular meetings.

"Ha!" you say. "No way." Time is tight, travel schedules are demanding, and your core team has their "day jobs." And these day-job responsibilities take lots of time and effort. What to do?

I have had great success with regular, monthly, two-hour meetings. These should be in-person—avoid videoconferencing if at all possible because you want to create a sense of urgency and deadline pressure. In-person meetings result in immediacy and face-to-face interaction, creativity, and a sense of *esprit* that can only come from your key players' being in the same room, at the same time, under the leader's watchful eye.

Is time availability a major issue? Fine. Link the monthly new product development (NPD) meeting to divisional meetings, in order to enhance time efficiencies.

To communicate the importance of your innovation effort, you need to make time for these meetings, and make sure everyone on the team understands that they *will* happen, and that participation *is* mandatory and that there are no excuses for lateness, unpreparedness, and a lack of participation.

The CEO or designated leader runs the meetings. Prior to each session, this program champion will discuss key issues and build consensus and help make decisions, with select members of the team.

Why, you ask? Innovation can be contentious. Innovation and NPD programs can create conflicts. Financial concerns. Manufacturing issues. Marketing approaches. Things have to mesh, and each key element of the equation has to be addressed by the champion—not just "manufacturability."

Progress reports are mandatory. Each meeting will monitor progress, address issues and concerns, share research and results, and allow for recalibration of priorities. New decisions will be made. Customer needs and wants will have to be considered. And, as stated previously, innovation objectives will be created and prioritized for the next 30 days—in congruence with overall business objectives. It's all about accountability (another step in Robert's Rules), and the leader needs to ensure that project-by-project timelines and investment decisions are on track.

Productivity at these meetings will depend largely on the composition of the team and complexity of the product line(s). So part of the leadership function is a determination of who is on the team. In my experience, many midsized and smaller companies have a limited number of internal experts from which to choose. The CEO runs the show. Key players should then include captains from sales, finance, operations, and marketing. And for those of you at larger firms: It's still your inspiration that drives the process and sets the tone.

The net takeaway? In time, a new, vibrant culture is developed, one that runs throughout the organization. Do it right, step by step, building consensus, reinforcing ideas, underscoring the need for accountability, asking the right questions. Don't rush it—it will come.

But don't waver, either. Stick to your guns, remain consistent, and it will happen. Thanks to you, the one who inspires.

For further information on this topic, be sure to check out Chapters 4, 5, and 8.

## No Risk, No Innovation

All-Star Joe Mauer of the Minnesota Twins led Major League Baseball in 2009 with a lofty batting average of .365. In second place was the amazing Ichiro Suzuki of the Seattle Mariners, batting .352. This means that Mauer *failed* to hit 63.5 percent of the time. Ichiro *failed* 64.8 percent of the time. But failure is not what they're thinking about when they're up at the plate. They have a plan to execute and they work out a quality at-bat.

Similarly, there is a success ratio when it comes to innovation. One recent example: A study on the grocery business (www.allbusiness.com) pegs the success rate for new product entries at 1:100. *One percent.* A company's appetite for failure during difficult financial times can shrivel with the realization that innovation means "outcome uncertainty."

It took Thomas Edison 6,000 tries to perfect and get to the incandescent light bulb.

Not every idea can, or will, be a winner. Not every *Eureka!* moment pans out. Consequently, innovation—and the budgets to support it—become big, fat, juicy targets. Champions of organizational innovation must have, and encourage, a *tolerance for failure* and *enthusiasm for risk taking.*

Without risk, there can be no innovation. In a tough economic environment, the willingness to take risk—given the cost of failure—can wither. But one can't pull the plug on an idea too soon.

An essential part of this dialogue is the element of trust. In my experience, teams perform best when they trust that failure will not result in punitive measures. Fear of failure can kill innovation. Your team will be afraid to act, decide, move forward, and do the work its capable of. Stasis.

Remember, too, that new ideas and technologies take time to gestate in the marketplace and take root with end users. Hybrid cars? How would they have fared in the late 1990s, when energy was relatively cheap and SUVs owned the roads of America?

And, all the while, management's hair turns gray and fingers twitch, waiting to pull the plug on this latest creation. But I recall the experience I had with foaming hand soap, which we introduced in 2000 and was fairly flat in the marketplace for more than three years until several key customers really "got" the concept and pushed it hard, into a variety of industry subsegments. The visual analysis in Exhibit 2.1 tells the story.

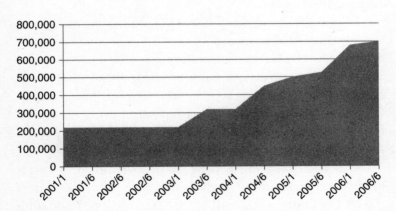

**Exhibit 2.1    Estimated U.S. Retail Hand Soap Sales (weekly unit sales)**

*Source:* Airspray N.V. based on retail sales data

At Airspray, we mapped out three-dimensional growth. That is, growth in geographic regions, new products, and new segments/applications. We took risks entering white spaces such as foaming candy, but the positive effect was remarkable, as first the inner box, and then the outer box, expanded. This approach, or philosophy, is called *innovation architecture* and is described in detail in the book *Innovation to the Core* by Peter Skarzynksi and Rowan Gibson (Harvard Business School Press, 2008).

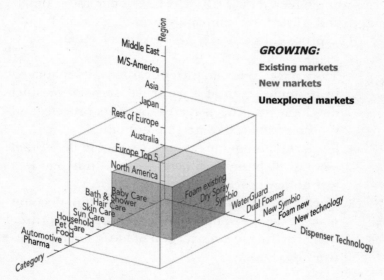

**Exhibit 2.2    Airspray Growth in 3-D**
*Source:* Rexam Airspray, B.V.

For further information on this topic, see Chapters 4, 5, and 8.

## New Product Development Process

A formalized New Product Development NPD process, frequently referred to as a Stage-Gate® Process,* is a must. The Stage-Gate innovation process is, according to its developers, "a carefully designed business process" and the result of comprehensive research into understanding the reasons behind product success and failure (see www.stage-gate.com for more information). The process was pioneered by Dr. Robert G. Cooper and is widely used, and trusted, by companies around the world.

The process, in essence, has two key elements:

1. The "stage" refers to the critical activities that need to be undertaken at a particular stage of product development. This is a cross-business process, and requires balanced ownership by multiple functions. Stage content, in my experience, should be divided among all business functions—it is not purely a technology process.
2. The "gating" process involves ownership, decision makers, degree of flexibility, criteria, and prioritization. This includes a selection of ideas and concepts from the hopper.

Overall, it is important to note that the NPD process must be a cross-business function. Therefore, all business functions must be aware of the process. Communication of relevant information is essential. Key personnel should be involved in the go/no-go gating reviews.

---

*Stage-Gate® is a registered trademark of Product Development Institute Inc.

As for the reviews, these should be shared internally. Further, metrics are essential to demonstrate progress and create/encourage momentum and internal enthusiasm. Establishment of a mix of input metrics (such as average time in each stage), and output metrics, such as the value of launched products, percentage of new product sales, and so on, provides a balanced scorecard for innovation. Additionally, a streamlined, or "express" version of the process can be utilized for line extensions, to accelerate progress.

As an aside, I asked long-time associate and new product developer Jeff DeFazio how to determine whether one's NPD process is up to snuff. He notes that "if sales of new products are less than 15 percent of total sales, check the composition of your innovation team, revisit your organization's culture, and execute an informal self-audit that examines the type of new products you're developing, the frequency of new product launches, and outside perceptions of your company."

As for the format for the NPD process, this can be as simple as an Excel spreadsheet, or matrix, or as detailed as the formal processes in Chapter 7, Innovation Implementation, with as many as six stages, simultaneous processes, go/no-go decisions, and so on.

But even basic NPD efforts require a monthly updating and reprioritization. Such a straightforward approach typically includes:

- Idea generation and screening
- Concept development and business analysis
- Prototype development
- Scale-up/commercialization
- Launch
- Tracking and measurement

According to DeFazio, "It's better to spend more time up front in creating the NPD process, as this front-loading results in less time and wasted energy later on." Typically, he said, innovation teams try to take up-front shortcuts and lose sight of the key goal of innovation: profitable growth.

The key purpose of the NPD pipeline is to create a structured, transparent process that allows management of project groups, DeFazio explained. And the key elements include quality, capability, and capacity.

- In terms of *quality*, the innovation team strives to select projects that, if successful, will deliver the best strategic outcome for the invested funds.
- For *capability*, the process helps track how effectively an individual project is managed and allowed to progress.
- *Capacity* refers to how the business manages and prioritizes resources supporting a portfolio of well-managed (or "capable") projects.

Remember what I mentioned in Chapter 1: Fail fast, but fail cheap. The institution of a proper NPD process will enhance your idea-to-launch methodology. Gates with "teeth" will help go/kill decision making and prioritization, define the gatekeepers, and provide a systematic approach to gatekeeping behavior. (See Exhibit 2.3.)

Further, portfolio management will be simplified and flexible enough to achieve the optimal balance and mix of products in the hopper. Success criteria at the gates will be concretized, and, ideally, a financial overlay will further help prioritize projects against available resources.

Institution of a robust postlaunch review is another key element in the process. Establishment of performance

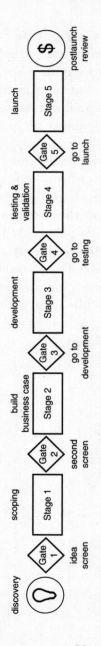

**Exhibit 2.3   The Quintessential Stage-Gate Flowchart**

*Source:* Stage-Gate®. Stage-Gate is a registered trademark of Product Development Institute Inc.

metrics measure how well a specific new product project performed. This is a powerful aid to understanding and analyzing results and learning how to improve future projects (see the next section, Ownership). Star-Gate is one of many forms of a formal step-by-step NPD process options to use and apply. Some of the others to consider include PDMA and SETR.

What about the front end of the process, the so-called funnel? Many organizations now modify the front end of the NPD process to feature more opportunity for experimentation. At the same time, they rely less on *financial* go/kill criteria, and more on *strategic* go/kill criteria.

Time to get specific. The flowcharts in Chapter 7 and Appendices A, B, and C will help you visualize exactly how an NPD program might work for your company. There, you'll see how we take our "wild idea" from a gleam in the eye (*dream*), through the *discovery* phase, to *design*, then *development*, and, finally, *delivery*.

**Ownership**

Innovation needs ownership, a champion within the organization. The champion must convince others to take calculated risks and work a bit—okay sometimes a lot—outside of one's comfort zone.

Often, the most successful product development managers are the most facile, accomplished, and successful salespeople within the company. Why? Because, as the leader, sometimes you have to be able to build consensus around a new, untested idea and have a disparate group of people, who typically are highly resistant to change, rally for a cause with an uncertain outcome.

I spoke recently with a CEO of a consumer products company who expressed his disappointment—he had an idea for an exciting new wrinkle in sunglasses technology, but his company stumbled and was beaten to market by others.

"I was the leader," he said, "and I guess I failed to sell it in. Despite the unique opportunity, the others just didn't get it. So everyone executed, in a manner of speaking. But their hearts weren't in it. They were moving forward out of duty, not out of passion. And we dropped the ball."

And that's the owner's job, when it comes to innovation. To marshal forces, empower, inspire, get the team members to be stakeholders in the success, to have and inspire the passion to get the best outcome.

There are certain realities we need to face. Even with proper ownership, sometimes teams just don't work all that well in the NPD environment. The participants can be easy to criticize—juicy targets for corporate negativity should a project not come to fruition.

Some participants are risk averse. They will not feel comfortable taking a stand that (they believe) could potentially be embarrassing, unpopular, or—worse—career damaging. Some folks just plain don't like to make decisions and take a passive-aggressive approach to interpersonal relationships.

All the more reason for each product development project to have a powerful leader/owner who is a company-wide champion for the effort, the leading advocate, and, possibly, ultimate decision maker. Ideally, a team leader should also be a team member of other efforts, to enhance cross-fertilization of experience and knowledge. In addition to accountability, this cross-participation in multiple NPD efforts enhances mutual respect and support for each other's efforts.

Who should be the owner/champion? Ideally, he or she should be an officer or executive/management member, with respect, authority, and the time and passion to make things happen, to drive the project forward.

However, he or she can also be a manager of a larger organization, especially if this individual is respected and has growth potential. Product managers with a strong understanding of their line are great candidates.

The size of the group is important as well. For a line extension, perhaps three to five team members is a good workable number, not too big or too small. Nimble, able to turn on a dime. Clearly, the optimal size of the group is subjective but, in my experience, nimbler is better and less is more.

Rather than obsessing about the size of the group, however, I'd stress the importance of maintaining regular, organized team meetings, with clearly defined objectives. Key points to remember are:

- Face to face (in person) is best.
- Keep a regular date, time, and duration.
- Clearly state meeting objectives in a written, pre-distributed agenda.
- Include cross-functional teams: marketing, sourcing, purchasing, sales, operations, quality assurance, and so on.
- All participants to update their responsibilities in advance of meeting.
- Review NPD by priority level (high/medium/low).
- Set next steps and a clear-cut action plan, follow through, and instill accountability.

For further information on this topic, see Chapters 4, 6, and 8.

**Value Creation**

Successful innovation turns ideas into money. All the processes, all the creativity, all the time and effort and research and dreaming and refining and modeling and retesting—what's it all for?

To enhance stakeholder value. To build incremental revenues, by filling a consumer need. And burnish your brand in the process.

Customer value can be created through the actual value-added of the new product, once you find that delicate balance between cost, price, and return. It is essential to get customer input and feedback during development, in order to create—ideally—a launching customer.

Important, too, is the interrelationship among cost, manufacturability, and end-user or consumer perceived value. Value can be seen in the very medium of the product. A perfect example: the foaming hand soap developed by my Airspray firm. The older, liquid hand soaps were a household staple for decades—convenient, or more convenient, that is, than bar soaps.

But liquids were not the ultimate medium consumers wanted, as history would prove. Foam is what they really wanted, and the perceived value of the instant-foam hand soap at first surprised all the industry experts in terms of the velocity of worldwide demand.

This is my cue to segue into the importance of understanding consumer drivers and of doing a good job in market assessment, mapping the competition, and weighing benefits versus price. Consumer or user input should be considered at several key junctions along the path to NPD, but be careful regarding heavy weighting of consumer focus groups very early on in the process. To quote my long-time Dutch colleague, Edgar van der Heijden, "Consumers can't imagine what they don't know."

As for stakeholder value, this comes in two ways, first as return on investment (ROI), then through enhanced product value. Longer-term, enhanced product value begets higher margins, greater returns, and superior company valuation, through the careful nurturing of your organization's intellectual property (IP) portfolio.

Innovation IP is protected through patents. Patents protect and define the innovation and are the key step on the way to commercialization and enhancing value. It is imperative that, in the quest for enhanced value through innovation, companies protect their technology and expertise through aggressive patenting programs.

Renew, refresh, and update regularly with new patents. Despite the expense, it is more than worthwhile; the solid sale price for Airspray was largely based on our patent portfolio and value. Patenting is a powerful value driver.

For further information on this topic, see Chapter 6.

## Accountability

Action items that don't get done. Incentives that don't work. NPD programs that lose traction, despite the best, brightest, most passionate innovation owners. It's a frustrating thing, when the process becomes akin to "herding cats."

And that is why one of the most important of Robert's Rules of Innovation is *Accountability*.

Accountability is a critical component of the trust equation. From the outset, every member of the team has to swear, in blood if that's what it takes, to hold to deadlines, to be accountable to each other, to other departments, to outside forces.

With the NPD process, the innovation team is like a group of mountaineers, led by you, the steadfast Sherpa guide, all of you tethered by the same length of rope. No one should feel comfortable slipping up.

So let's go back to the regular NPD meetings we're scheduling. Clear action items should come from each monthly meeting. Team members must follow through on agreed-upon assignments. Should a "day-job" responsibility make deadlines a problem, it is that teammate's responsibility to alert others well ahead of time, so that coverage on that assignment is possible and progress continues.

Team members need to feel responsibility for delivery. If laying on guilt is what it takes, so be it. Slippage is the sure way to jeopardize the entire NPD process—and the corporate image. The impact of process failures is both internal and external.

A word here about the creative mind-set. In my opinion, creative people *can* be organized and encouraged to stick to schedules. I also believe that organized people can be extremely creative.

Sound heretical? I recognize that this is not the popular wisdom. But I have seen plenty of left-brain/right-brain people in my worldwide experience, and I can tell you with assurance: People with good hearts and strong minds, who feel responsible for the outcome of a group project, will be able to handle their role within the NPD group.

Developers and researchers like to hobby, to noodle around with wonderful new ideas, and, yes, they need freedom to explore their inner Einstein. And the reality is, the success of your NPD initiatives hinges on that most fragile of attributes: creativity.

Creation loves chaos, and control is anathema to creativity, or so the theory goes. Think of all the artists, musicians, and designers who have that certain gift to create something wonderful from the magic that exists only between their ears. These folks are not the same as those who are perfectly happy punching the clock at 5 P.M. and watching reality-based television programs all night long.

Which is why we come back, at this point, to the role of the champion, who must infuse the group with the "one for all, all for one" mentality that served Alexander Dumas's Three Musketeers so well, and that will move your NPD program on to new heights. The champion is the key, the respected leadership model who encourages, supports, and facilitates cross-team participation.

Our recent survey of executives (see www.innovation coach.com for details) found that a sense of accountability is one of the "most difficult" things to create within organizational culture of any kind. Exhibit 2.4 shows the recent results.

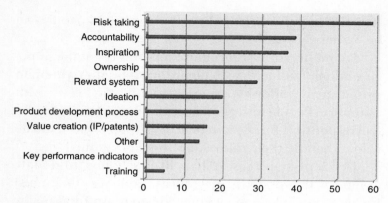

**Exhibit 2.4  Which Elements of an Innovation Process and/or Culture Are the Most Difficult to Put in Place?**

*Source*: www.innovationcoach.com.

I do favor some free time, some flexibility for your creatives' "skunk works" or pet side projects, as they're referred to in some of our most innovative firms. I would even encourage tying skunk work success with rewards. As long as everyone realizes *they're running a business*. Therefore, NPD team members—yes, all of them—need to be held accountable.

End of sermon.

For further information on these topics, see Chapters 4, 5, and 8.

**Training and Coaching**

Proper hiring, training, and coaching is the way to create, reinforce, and enhance company culture and mind-set. This attitude needs to come from the top, and, in our most admired firms, frequently represents the ethos of the founder. Human resources can work magic for your NPD efforts by helping you put the right people in the slots that suit them—and you.

Ongoing reinforcement of this attitude and spirit is essential, to help employees understand their place on the NPD team and give their best. Continuity is the key, while training helps your team constantly improve its skill set, through new techniques in ideation, process experience, and intraorganizational communication of best practices.

Innovative companies, by the way, are not necessarily created by establishing a discrete "Department of Innovation." On the contrary, it's important for *the company* to be innovative. These are organizations where being open-minded is a positive attribute, not a threat. In many industries, such as fashion and personal care products, the key company driver is "innovation." That is the common denominator, and it is frequently the mantra of the company founder, who creates and maintains—okay, *demands*—that unique culture. I have frequently found category leaders that develop centers of innovation, and train and retrain executives on project management basics.

And the basis of this successful innovation? A natural curiosity, open-mindedness, an ability to see the big picture—combined with hard-headed business acumen. Or, and it bears repeating, a left-brain/right-brain approach.

For further information on this topic, see Chapters 5 and 8.

**Idea Management**

Feed the beast. Pack the pipeline. Ideation, or idea management processes/system LTD (long-term development) is essential to the innovation effort. This is where the future's "wild ideas" come from, and it should be harnessed by a process with dedicated resources and with NPD and LTD teams working together.

Bear in mind that the funnel needs to be filled to "feed" NPD, but leadership—the CEO—needs to also consider separate LTD efforts. LTD has its own discrete R&D, testing and retesting, before concepts are winnowed down to viable NPD concepts that then make their way to the end of the funnel, as noted in the Stage-Gate model shown earlier.

*Ideation sessions*—the very term makes some executives roll their eyes derisively, even as it makes others chomp at the bit, in anticipation of the next session. The naysayers picture a room full of silliness, with flip-chart paper taped over the walls and windows, and staffers playing with crayons and children's toys. The proponents of the ideation session, frankly, see pretty much the same thing. That's what it frequently looks like.

Frequent, intelligently facilitated ideation sessions lead to successful new products. It's all about batting averages—a small percentage of concepts make it through the process. But what a payoff!

To get started, let's talk first in more general terms and then drill down to ideation session specifics.

In addition to your team, it's also valuable to include customers and/or sales members in your monthly or—at the very least—biannual ideation sessions. Customers, some claim, provide golden insights for the NPD/LTD teams. I'm of mixed mind about combining your people with your customer and their people at the same meeting (this is discussed further in Chapter 8); for now, suffice it to say that this practice can be inhibiting for your people, but I know for a fact that there are many who disagree with me.

Salespeople also have remarkable abilities to discuss marketplace nuances and "what-if" scenarios, even if some of them can't stop talking for even a minute. (Of course I jest, you sales folks out there.)

For ideation sessions, think about brainstorming, in addition to products and features, processes or technical changes. Be sure to include customer service, engineering, production, and other departments, in addition to your brainstorming session "usual suspects." Again, new perspectives are an asset to the process. It's always a shame when certain departments are considered "not very creative" and are excluded from ideation sessions. After all, in the final analysis, we're all consumers. It's all about the interplay between the extroverts and the quieter types, in a variety of environments, with the right kind of facilitator who artfully opens the discussion and allows freedom for everyone to speak, without fear of ridicule, condemnation, or worse.

And think of the negativity you've heard over the years at ideation sessions. Do any of these sound familiar?

"That will never work!"

"We tried that years ago; it was a disaster!"

"There's no way that can be built!"

"We don't have budget for *that!*"

At your ideation sessions, remember: there are no bad ideas. All concepts are written on the flip charts, whiteboards, and the like, and filed, prioritized, validated, for future reference and/or use in combination with other ideation session results.

What of the balance between NPD and LTD efforts? Many small companies grapple with this and mix NPD and LTD teams. To be blunt, I do not advocate this, although I do believe that resources should be mixed in NPD teams. But without dedicated LTD resources, staff tends to get buried in NPD activity, in my experience, without the needed perspectives on long-term development ideas and reality checks on manufacturability.

Getting back to ideation sessions, we've all seen incredibly lively groups and groups that are just flat dead. There are many variables to ideation outcomes, as you are dealing with people who have real lives, with problems, distractions, and "day jobs" that need attention. It's important to encourage initial "creative play" but to not overplan and overprop the session. The magic frequently comes from the facilitator's people skills.

A diverse group at the ideation session is ideal. Diversity provides the social tension needed for a quality outcome. Also, be aware of the time of day. First thing on Monday morning—no way. Also not the most productive are late on Friday afternoon or right after lunch, when energy levels drop.

Make sure your team has at least some connection to the product—has either used it, or sold it, or assembled it. This is especially important for the facilitator of the session.

Here are some additional tips for facilitators:

- *Stack the deck*. Prior to the session, ask each group member to write down a self-description in only five or six words. This gives the facilitator insight into the participants and helps him or her stack the deck a little to ensure superior results.

- *Break up teams.* Select people who may know each other but are not "that friendly" with each other, in order to minimize group-think.
- *Vary the format.* Predictable times, formats, rooms, can deaden ideation sessions—mix it up to keep people out of their comfort zones—try one at a customer's office.
- *It's all good.* Always accept every idea and get it written on the board; keep every scrap of paper for future reference "so we can live in the ideation moment, well after the session has ended."
- *Info alchemy.* Build a database of ideas, from which new combinations and solutions can be derived. One plus one plus one can equal 1,000 sometimes.
- *Keep it simple.* Ideation sessions can be complex, or they can be simple—both types can be effective. The key is for innovation champions to regularly remind the team.

Stay open to new ideas, read the relevant blogs, capture consumer insights—the showstoppers can come from anywhere.

For further information on these topics, see Chapters 5 and 7.

**Observe and Measure**

Observation, measurement, and tracking of NPD results are essential to optimal ROI. Create your baselines first, with initial observations and measurements. Then capture the time to each gate, the time spent inside each gate, and so on.

Look for improvements in terms of reduction of time spent within each gate. Once a product is launched, a key metric is the ratio of new product sales to overall sales. One method would be to track historical new product sales for the first three years after launch versus total sales. This is a baseline. Next, set a target goal for this ratio, based on your needs and taking into consideration your competitive environment and the competition's baseline. This would be further calibrated to account for the product lifestyle in a particular industry, but in any case, new product sales are measured as a percentage of the total.

It's fascinating to watch when you are making headway. You see your margins growing, as the right mix of new products come on-stream.

This step is all about continuous improvement. Plan. Do. Check. Act. Things won't always go as planned, so take corrective actions and make ongoing course corrections.

Product life cycles keep getting shorter and shorter, which mandates accelerated NPD cycles. In the personal care arena, for example, life cycles are only two to three years. So each big idea has tremendous potential value, and it's important not to kill a potential success too early.

Following are the top five R&D metrics used by industry (2008):[*]

---

[*]*Source:* Goldense Group Inc.'s 2008 Product Development Metrics Survey Base: 200 companies that design and develop new products, Discovered via ThomasNet's Industrial Market Trends.

1. R&D spending as a percentage of sales (77 percent).
2. Total patents filed/pending/awarded/rejected (61 percent).
3. Total R&D head count (59 percent).
4. Current-year percentage sales due to new products released in the past six years (56 percent).
5. Number of new products released (53 percent).

For additional recent survey results, see www.innovation coach.com/survey. For further information on this topic, see Chapters 3 and 7.

##  Net Result and Reward

When it's all said and done, innovation is about ROI derived from the alchemy of ideas to money. Everyone wins. With profitable growth come benefits to shareholders, stakeholders, employees, customers, and consumers—through market share gain, new products, and new features.

Yes, everyone wins, and accelerating the process is suitable financial reward for those who drive the NPD process to new heights. In my experience, many have benefited from remuneration packages that reward the head of R&D via a percentage of sales from new products.

Remember, too, that incentives are needed for all participants, and that includes your development staff. Frequently, the key motivator is less financial than it is recognition for their job well done, validation for their Zen-like ability to conjure new concepts and test and retest prototypes. So FYI: Motivation isn't always about money, but motivation is critical. Reward your people. They are your best innovation resource.

For further information on this topic, see Chapters 4 and 7.

### Think About

- How would you improve your current NPD process?
- Who is your organization's innovation champion? How would you rate his or her ability?
- Are your team meetings (1) regular, (2) in-person, and (3) productive?
- Is your NPD pipeline as robust as you'd like it to be?

# 3

# The Innovation Audit

## THE INVALUABLE DISCOVERY PROCESS THAT SETS THE STAGE FOR ACTION

By now you understand the opportunity inherent in sustainable innovation, and you have reviewed Robert's Rules of Innovation. You suspect that the time to start has arrived. But how do you know for sure that it is time to commit to the time and effort it takes to push forward with a program of sustainable innovation?

Perhaps there are new competitive reasons for such an effort:

- A new player has emerged in your marketplace, or an older firm is on the verge of collapse, opening new opportunities you feel ill-equipped to capitalize.
- The percentage of total sales from your new product introductions is stagnant or has slipped.
- Profitability has softened and/or costs are spiraling.
- Recent product development programs have stalled or been beset by internal bickering. Perhaps they

always have been, but new competitive pressures now render such inefficiencies unacceptable.

- If yours is a public company, share price has fallen.

Bruce Sauter is a true innovator who brought great ideas and energy to the Kohler team, where we first worked together. He is also a long-time fan of the great writer Tennessee Williams, who wrote:

> It is almost as if you were frantically constructing another world, while the world that you live in dissolves beneath your feet, and that your survival depends on completing this construction at least one second before the old habitation collapses.
>
> www.bbc.co.uk/dna/h2g2/A337367

Perhaps you have that sense that the old order within your organization is changing and yet the new structure is not yet firm—and you have the unnerving feeling that you need to establish clear guidelines to determine where you are now. And measure this against future accomplishments.

But where do you begin? Remember *Alice in Wonderland:* "Begin at the beginning," the king said gravely, "and go on till you come to the end: then stop." With sustainable innovation, Sauter reminds us, we will indeed begin at the beginning. But there really is no end to the process, and it is folly to ever stop.

The process begins with a rigorous innovation audit, where we set a benchmark and priorities, which—let's face it—require ongoing course corrections over time.

## The Audit Process

In tackling the audit process, one is actually peering into the organization's innovation core, as Bruce Sauter so aptly expresses it. What is that core? "It's ideally a learning environment that nurtures and sustains creativity," he says. "This environment is supported and protected by a positive attitude, by imagination, and a bias toward action and passion."

"It is further supported by leadership's vision and a set of core values," Sauter says. He defines three separate and distinct forces: need, knowledge, and industry trends/ technology. These forces are shown in Exhibit 3.1. "From this," he says, "comes innovation."

There are two audit levels to consider:

1. A *short audit,* in which several key, fundamental questions are asked, which pertain directly to

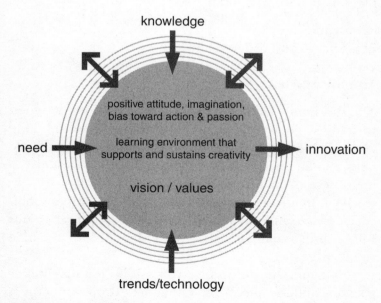

**Exhibit 3.1   Sauter Innovation Core**
*Source:* Bruce Sauter.

Robert's Rules of Innovation. This can easily be accomplished and provides a fine initial by way of a radar graph and assessment of strengths, weaknesses, and areas that must be addressed in creation of an innovation program.

2. The *in-depth audit,* a comprehensive discovery process in 10 main areas that leads to understanding of the current innovation scenario and sets the stage for the subsequent development of an action plan.

Working with an innovation coach/professional, these areas are identified to meet the needs of the individual organization, to ensure the most appropriate and applicable data collection and analysis.

With that overview, let's take a closer look at each type of audit.

## The Short Audit

The short audit is a series of yes-or-no questions designed to address your current toolbox and get you thinking about elements you'll need to create or bolster. A sample questionnaire is shown in Exhibit 3.2. Your honest assessment here is vital, so be brave.

If you complete the short audit online (www.innovation coach.com/solutions/short-audit/), the graphical results will be displayed immediately. See Exhibit 3.3 for a sample results page.

It's important not to beat yourself up too much after glancing at these questions. Rather, let's think about them together and place them in the context of Robert's Rules of Innovation, introduced in Chapter 2.

**Exhibit 3.2    Short Audit Questionnaire**

| | |
|---|---|
| Inspire | Is the strategic plan/corporate strategy in support of innovation? |
| | Does the executive leadership drive innovation? |
| | Is innovation in the hearts and minds of all employees involved? |
| Product Development | Have new product development process in place? |
| | Have a pipeline of products to develop? |
| | Launch new products in timely fashion? |
| Culture | Does the leadership team believe innovation to be the lifeblood of the company? |
| | Have clear set of metrics to track performance? |
| | Looking for continuous improvement? |
| Ideation | Have ideation process/methodology in place? |
| | Have definition for success criteria? |
| | Proper evaluation and criteria to kill ideas? |
| Reward | New product objectives clearly set? |
| | Rewards and recognition program in place? |
| | Is risk taking and failure acceptable with the company? |

*Source:* www.innovationcoach.com.

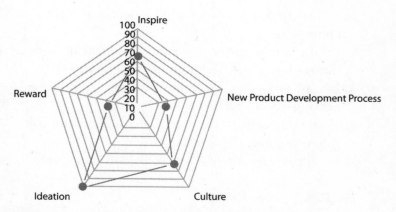

**Exhibit 3.3    Short Audit Radar Chart Sample Result**
*Source:* www.innovationcoach.com.

## The In-Depth Audit

There are two types of in-depth audits: online and on-site.

Ideally, the online in-depth innovation audit should take place first, and the on-site audit should follow. This allows further exploration of the online results and questions.

### The Online In-Depth Audit

Allows you to get a more detailed picture of your current score based on the 10 imperatives of Robert's Rules of Innovation (Chapter 2) as opposed to a rough assessment of the short audit. The *on-site in-depth innovation audit*, as a follow-up, covers three key areas: strategy, process, and organization. Whether online or in person, these questions need to be answered with the chief innovation officer and other key members of the leadership team.

Sample questions include:

### Inspire

1. Is the business leader the innovation driver or champion?
2. Do the leader and senior management team believe innovation is the lifeblood of the company?
3. Is your vision for innovation inspiring, acting as a rallying cry for all associates?
4. Is there an active culture of dialogue between roles, functions, and departments?
5. Have you identified your innovation blockers?

### No Risk . . . No Reward

1. Do you allow free research-and-development (R&D) time?

2. Do you invest in innovation: money, people, resources?

3. Do you require return on investment (ROI) on each project?

4. Do you "celebrate" failure and risk taking?

5. Are you open to ideas from the outside?

## New Product Development (NPD) Process

1. Do you have a defined product development process?

2. Do you apply go/no-go decision points?

3. Do you have at least monthly review meetings?

4. Do you prioritize projects regularly?

5. Do you always launch innovations in a timely manner?

## Ownership

1. Do you have champions that own projects?

2. Is there an ownership culture in the company?

3. Do NPD teams have champions? At what level of the organization?

4. Is it clear who the "go to" resource is for innovation?

5. Is there a central and unified picture of your innovation efforts?

## Value Creation

1. Do you track what percentage of sales is new products?

2. Do you have a minimum threshold that new products must render in operating profit or gross margin?

3. Intellectual property: Do you have or file for patents?

4. Do you have a deep enough understanding of your customer needs and have avenues to get the insight and input?
5. Do you measure financial success?

## Accountability

1. Is there accountability in the organization?
2. Is there a high level of candor and trust?
3. Is there accountability in the NPD process, actions/to-do follow-through?
4. Do you define action items at the end of each product development review meeting?
5. Is it clear to specific individuals and groups what their responsibilities are?

## Training and Coaching

1. Do you have an ongoing training program in place?
2. Do you coach champions/project leaders?
3. Do you have standardized project management in place?
4. Do you share best practices among teams?
5. Do you constantly look for new ways to improve your products and processes, even the successful ones?

## Ideation

1. Do you have an ideation method in place?
2. Do you manage the ideas in the hopper (re-evaluation, prioritization, cross-fertilization, etc.)?
3. Do you have multiple avenues to get customer insight and input?
4. Do you apply evaluation criteria to help you identify the best ideas?

**5.** Do you have dedicated long-term development resources (separate from NPD)?

### Observe and Measure

**1.** Do you measure what percentage of your income comes from products less than five years old?
**2.** Do you measure new product sales?
**3.** Do you have a set of metrics to serve as an innovation dashboard and track your innovation activities?
**4.** Do you have and maintain new product key performance indicators?
**5.** Do you track R&D spending or head count?

### Net Result and Reward

**1.** Do you track new product sales objectives?
**2.** Do you reward people who contribute good ideas to the organization?
**3.** Do you have a reward system in place for creativity?
**4.** Do you recognize staff for creativity and accomplishments of NPD?
**5.** Do you have a new product sales bonus?

How did you fare? What about in the context of the spider chart shown in Exhibit 3.4?

Bear in mind that such a process is enriching, even if you found that many of your responses indicate room for improvement. As I mentioned earlier, this is part of a self-awareness process that will help set the groundwork for what comes next.

### The On-Site In-Depth Audit

As I mentioned in the previous section, there are three key areas involved in this process:

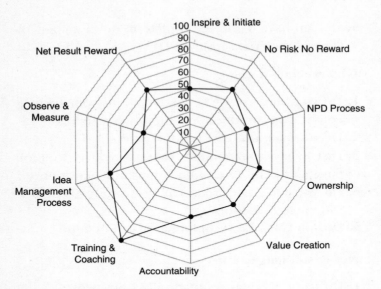

**Exhibit 3.4  Spider Chart—10 Imperatives**
*Source:* www.innovationcoach.com.

1. Innovation strategy
2. Innovation process
3. Innovation organization

The on-site audit begins with an organizational overview, a summary of general attributes, which often includes questions such as:

- How many people do you employ?
- How many locations do you have? In how many countries?
- How many product lines do you have? Services? Distinct manufacturing processes?
- What is your organizational structure? What is the relationship between management, finance, and R&D?

- What are three adjectives that describe your organization *as you now envision it?*
- Do you currently have an innovation strategy?
  - If so, describe it briefly.
  - If not, do you plan to establish one? What is the plan you envision?
- What are the five aspects of your organization that you believe are the *least* innovative?
- Why do you want your organization to be more innovative?
- How do you think your organization could improve its potential for innovation?
- Do you have any additional comments or insights that would help analyze your current innovation scenario?

Whether you address these questions with an outside, third-party professional or in-house, the mere process of thinking about your responses can go a long way to getting you on the right track and ready to create an innovation action plan.

Now let's examine the individual components of the assessment.

**Part I: Innovation Strategy**   An appropriate assessment of your innovation strategy must provide a comprehensive view of current and future organic growth ambitions and platforms. Why? Your innovation strategy needs to create the linkage, or glue, between your business-driven innovation ambition and a portfolio focused on future value generation. To truly have a long-term commitment, innovation has to be part of the overall strategy, vision, and mission of the company.

As many as four approaches can be used to provide a full perspective on your strategy. These include looking at:

- *Strategic growth plan and alignment.* The goal is to identify existing organic growth targets and innovation-related implications across the company, product lines, or business units. Primary inputs are the current strategy plan or annual marketing plan, depending on the availability and size of the company, as well as interviews with innovation and/or strategy decision makers. The primary outputs include summaries of the existing organic growth strategy, the role of innovation, and delivery mechanisms. This will demonstrate/measure the current importance of innovation to enterprise growth and the part innovation activities are to play.

- *Innovation objectives and key performance indicators (KPIs).* This assessment identifies the existence and linkage of key innovation to business performance targets and any KPIs already in place and/or in the process of being implemented or reviewed. Typically use existing business unit targets, KPI summaries, and historical performance data, which show the effectiveness of the linkage of innovation results and activities.

- *Innovation portfolio and portfolio management.* Reviewing the current innovation spending and projects across the company. Review current product lines, strategic importance, and alignment and emphasis in the current innovation efforts. This process results in mapping of innovation projects and strategic alignment. In addition, one should test/validate the proper and/or assigned resources. No clear resources, no results. Such an approach will show where and how future innovation-driven growth will be delivered, and will reveal key strategic gaps.

- *Performance benchmarks.* Such activity is extremely valuable in terms of establishing benchmarks versus the competition and best practices. However, the ability to conduct this activity is wholly dependent upon the industry and accessibility of the relevant information.

**Part II: Innovation Process** This part of the in-depth audit helps analyze and interpret the organization's historic innovation delivery performance, and gauge the effectiveness of the process. Tools that provide insights into both internal and external factors include:

- *Idea–concept–launch performance.* Here, the key objective is to identify the historic performance of internal processes from concept to market, as well as the ratio of breakthrough versus incremental innovation. This is accomplished first by looking at hard facts and the new products introduced, and complemented with interviews with project champions.

- *Process effectiveness.* This assesses the process from ideation to market introduction. It looks into the effectiveness and content of the various stages, the teeth of the gates. It looks for both enablers and barriers to the process—and opportunities for improvement. Evaluate how well innovation projects are supported and championed throughout the process, from ideation to implementation.

- *Open innovation review.* This provides a clear view of how external sources of innovation are used by the organization. The process helps identify how well the company exploits its external network for both innovation sourcing and capitalizing on opportunities.

**Part III: Innovation Organization**   The ideal innovation team is knowledgeable, empowered, and motivated to drive ideation and product development. The innovation organization assessment helps identify the current and likely future capability of the company to deliver innovation that matches organizational and marketplace potential:

- *Innovation culture.* This part provides a view of internal perceptions of innovation culture across the organization. It looks at the inspirational drivers, communication, and ownership by associates. Trust and tolerance for failure are factors being looked at and considered.
- *Innovation organizational alignment.* The organizational alignment must support innovation goals and objectives. Further, it must open communications and identify champions key insights, such as reward and recognition, are identified.
- *Individual and group capability analysis.* For companies seeking effective, sustained innovation, it is crucial to have the right people and teams in place. So we look at the ability of the organization and key individuals within it to deliver desired results.

## The Importance of Establishing a Benchmark

The establishment of a benchmark is a critical element for those serious about sustainable innovation. It provides an objective and realistic view of where innovation stands within your organization compared to the outside world and in particular your peers—but also best in class. Why this differentiation? Often, companies will do benchmarking within their industry and establish their goals based on these findings. However, if the peer group or industry as a whole is not "best in class" and another industry does it better, the peer benchmark is just not robust enough.

Benchmarking is a key way to create a competitive advantage, and can be the avenue toward best practices that can or should be applied.

It's important, I believe, for an outside, thoroughly objective, third party to work with you on this vital first step of assessing the state of your innovation programs. After all, the benchmark is the key determinant in shaping all future innovation initiatives—in terms of team building, processes, management decisions, and more.

Without the establishment of the benchmark, unclouded by your emotional involvement, future assessment of your sustainable innovation program is difficult at best. You're driving without a global positioning system (GPS) or, at the very least, a printed road map.

It's reality versus perception, which underscores the importance of the noninvolved third-party assessment. Your innovation program may need only a few tweaks; you may not be as outgunned as you think. Or your program may need major surgery when, all along, you thought you were "almost there." Outside, impartial perspectives are invaluable.

When the benchmark is conducted, it is important to examine specific areas of your business, and take a "snapshot" of the current state of each. Such areas include the marketplace environment, recent product introductions, your organization's culture, the status of the current innovation team, and the mind-set of your organization's leadership.

Such a snapshot, fixed in time, will let you see where your organization is now, and help set a course for where you ultimately want to be, in terms of innovation culture, ideation, and new product development. The ideal benchmark process will provide an assessment of your overall innovation ability, an analysis of relative abilities of different departments and/or divisions, and a document that details specific areas for improvement, as well as enumerates organization strengths that can be built upon.

The audit process can be exhilarating, difficult, disappointing, encouraging—all at the same time. It is a demanding process. And it has to get done, if the organization is to understand where it is now, relative to where it can be, and to identify areas that are in good shape and that need remedy.

Bruce Sauter's innovation continuum, shown in Exhibit 3.5, helps leaders visualize where their organization is, in terms of its approach to innovation.

As you work with your innovation coach and/or internal innovation SWAT team to map your organization's position in the world of sustainable innovation, think about Sauter's continuum and try to identify where you currently are in the spectrum, and where you would like to be:

*Dinosaur:* Chooses to compete in places less affected by change; has inactive innovation capability.

*Catch-up:* Always in a position of having to catch up with other industry players; in reactive mode.

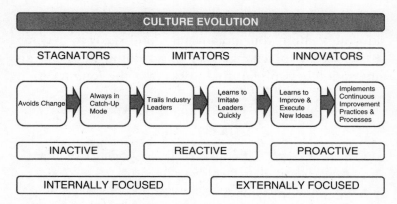

**Exhibit 3.5    Innovation Continuum Slide**
*Source:* Bruce Sauter.

*Laggard:* Tries hard to innovate, but usually lags behind the leaders; in reactive mode.

*Imitator:* Great at copying the leaders' innovations; is quick and nimble, but still in reactive mode.

*Adaptor:* Can adapt new ideas readily and improves; is in proactive mode, but not the leader.

*Creator:* Continuously creates new ideas and leading-edge practices.

Think, too, about seriously forging a path that frees you from naysayers in the organization, from "Anti Bodies" types, doomsday scenario specialists who (fearful of change at best, and experts at innovation sabotage at worst) work to undermine previous innovation efforts at every turn.

Whether you address these questions with an outside, third-party professional or in-house, the mere process of thinking about your responses can go a long way to getting you on the right track and ready to face the devil's advocates within your organization and ready to become a true agent for change and in so doing to create an innovation action plan that works over the long term.

### Think About

- On Bruce Sauter's innovation continuum—from Dinosaur to Creator—where is your organization?
- What was the result of your most recent innovation audit?
- What has changed since that time? Internally? Externally?
- Have you identified a qualified third-party to help guide your innovation audit process?

# 4

# Innovation Emancipation

## KEYS TO FREEING YOUR INNER INNOVATOR

For my international network of colleagues and me, this is the topic that *really* gets us enthused. This chapter addresses the issue of *inspiration* and how the innovator-in-chief needs to truly champion this culture and drive it throughout the organization and make it happen, often in the face of fierce opposition, remembering the immortal words of Sir Winston Churchill: "A pessimist sees the difficulty in every opportunity; an optimist sees the opportunity in every difficulty."

## Defeating Devil's Advocates to Become an Agent for Change

Why do innovation efforts fail? One big reason is that sometimes the innovation strategy is working at cross-purposes with business strategy. Another reason is that innovation program goals may be unclear or measured inefficiently.

But many of the key reasons for derailed innovation programs tie back to culture- and people-related issues. As my colleagues would say regarding successful innovation:

- Know your markets cold.
- Move fast, but mostly. . . .
- Spend the time to find fantastic people.

It's difficult to be an agent for change when human nature compels your teammates to resist that very change and stick tenaciously to the status quo, which is much more comfortable and safe. It is very hard to defeat organizational devil's advocates who claim to want the best for the organization even as they work backchannels to dismantle plans to ratchet up innovation programming.

That is why innovation democratization is critical and why building company-wide consensus and developing multiple champions throughout the organization are the keys to creating a culture of innovation that sticks and meets your organization's business objectives.

*BusinessWeek* surveyed the top-ranked companies for innovation—including Apple, Google, 3M, Toyota, and Microsoft—and they all in part attributed their success to avoidance of these culture-related innovation pitfalls:

- Innovation that is "lip service"—all talk, no support
- Isolated innovation initiatives—no ongoing culture of innovation
- Fragmentation of the process—no organization-wide buy-in
- Resources concentrated by certain innovation blocs

So how does one truly champion an innovation culture? How does one defeat these legions of devil's advocates and drive innovation to new heights? What are the tips to become an effective agent for change within the organization?

We first asked Harlan F. Weisman, MD, chief science and technology officer, Medical Devices & Diagnostics, Johnson & Johnson. He is an expert on creating an environment for innovation, within which people can flourish, and he has authored more than 90 journal articles and book chapters in the fields of cardiovascular disease and medical product development.

"Today, it's innovate or die," he said. "Not just in health care, but throughout the business world." And yet, he notes, despite the innovation imperative, numerous obstacles interfere with the process.

"The key is creating teams across disciplines," he explains. "Get people to work together, across business units, geographical areas, cultures."

Entrepreneurs can have a "soloist's" state of mind—you know, "I can do it all." I know, because I was once one of these Lone Rangers, earlier in my career. But I believe Dr. Weisman, and I think you will, too, when he says, "A single inventor, alone, can't do it. Too much complexity. Sometimes you stop and say, 'Maybe it's just easier to come up with the big idea myself.' I'm here to tell you, it's not."

## Innovation Democratization Is the Key

The key, as Dr. Weisman puts it, is "convergence"—linking groups that wouldn't typically work together. People from different business groups, with different skill sets, from different backgrounds. In a word, *diversity*. You want an environment where not everybody thinks the same way, he says. "Mix people from different business units, geographic regions," he says. "Make sure the group has both men and women, and people from different ethnic groups, different age groups, and from a variety of functions.

"And the bigger the innovation, the more of a showstopper it is, the more this is necessary," Dr. Weisman says. "Remember, the chance of failure is far more likely than success, especially in my industry, pharma, where a great success ratio might be 1 out of 100."

"The answers," he continues, "are not always obvious and the paths to success not always linear. Thus, the need for a team that comes together, from different backgrounds, for a common purpose." Why? A typical methodology in problem solving, he says, is to assemble a top-ranked team of "the usual suspects"—people with a portfolio of success in a given field. These people, he says, can be driven by their past glory when, sometimes, what one needs is a group with a fresh slant, a blank slate.

Again, the question begs: why? The team of "usual suspects" may immediately take an existing solution to the next level, an incremental benefit, but not necessarily the home run. So how do we create the teamwork that can result in a showstopper, or what can be called "disruptive technology"? An even more daunting question is how to create a culture of innovation, an environment where a group of highly motivated, imaginative professionals actually become comfortable with the ambiguity needed to drop their defenses and work, together, toward the common goal of nailing that breakthrough idea.

The champion or driver, of the process first has to do a bit of self-analysis, and then look carefully at the composition of the team.

"If the group is composed of those who place their self-interest above the needs of the team, it just won't work,"

Dr. Weisman says. "And, in my experience, these people show themselves early on."

What about the characteristics of the team leader? Here's where a dose of self-awareness comes into play. As I said, many entrepreneurial types have a "superman" attitude—we can do it all, we don't need help. The thing of it is, in creating a culture of innovation, *help* is not a four-letter word.

Can you really say, and do you really believe, in your heart of hearts, that you are comfortable enough in your own skin to be challenged by those in your team? Are you really capable of facilitating an innovation meeting, encouraging new directions, asking the prompting question that leads to an exciting and different train of thought? Or are you really more comfortable dictating terms? Monopolizing the discussion? Heavy-handedly steering the group in the direction you prefer?

Here's the reality: The champion, the innovation driver, has to create an environment of trust and openness, where it's not just okay to take risks, but rather where it's critical for players to take risks. "It's not keeping score," Dr. Weisman says. "It's not 'who won and who lost.' It's letting the mental energy flow, and it requires ego strength, self-awareness, hard work, and the ability to bite one's tongue. You have to be able to actually encourage flops."

The champion also has to be able to weigh, understand, and be able to work with, the various factors that impact team members' professional lives. Dr. Weisman notes that "these folks still have their 'day jobs' and are beholden to their 'other bosses.'"

Additionally, people—being people—act in different ways while in a group setting, he cautions. "Some people just avoid conflict at any cost," he says. "Some act in classic passive-aggressive fashion. Others are overt, Type-A personalities that can easily take over a meeting." It's thus up to the champion, he notes, to break down barriers to resistance and get everyone playing nicely—and, more importantly, productively, in the proverbial "sandbox."

And sandbox is actually a decent metaphor, because one of the aspects of setting the right cultural tone is the ability of the leader to get back to the open, more elemental and innocent methods of the child, versus the well-defended interpersonal methodology of many adults.

"Talk to a preschooler; ask that child for their idea or opinion about virtually anything," Dr. Weisman says. "They'll give you their thinking, even when they have no idea what they're talking about. But the point is, they're very free, open, and giving. Their imaginations run free, without inhibition. That's the type of comfort you want to create—an environment where team members will be comfortable enough to take a risk and lose that adult blandness some of us exhibit in everyday lives. Let them, freely, act like kids."

One big way to do that is to establish an environment where the constraints are taken off. In terms of coming up with the game-breaking idea, what would "it" look like if there were no budget constraints, marketing issues, or production concerns. Freeing the team from very real-world issues can open up the dialogue and, of course, as leader you can always dial those budget-marketing-production constraints back in. Once the dialogue is opened up, it is then up to the leader, or innovation champion, to set the proper tone and facilitate.

And as we know from our everyday professional experience, meeting facilitation requires patience, restraint, intelligence, and good-natured shepherding. The leader will have to:

- Build team consensus for the project, or risk non-participation in some quarters (and yet, the good leader will assume all players have the best of intentions).
- Trust people even before they earn your precious trust; and not make your trust contingent upon proving loyalty to your ideas alone.
- Understand the diversity of perspectives in the room and that people may feel uncomfortable working with "the other"—those they wouldn't ordinarily work with.
- Realize that highly motivated professionals are not comfortable with not knowing "the answer."
- Devise a way to create a "safe haven" environment to coax the best out of the quieter members of the group; there will be those who have great ideas but will be reticent about piping up.
- Direct conversational traffic: some may try to "talk over" others, who politely wait for a pause in the conversation to interject—and this pause may not come without your help.
- Open dialogues and collaborative relationships with local business groups, suppliers, customers, and universities.

Dr. Weisman steadfastly believes that this approach to creating a productive environment for innovation that cuts across traditional barriers and territoriality helps create solutions more easily, as well as create solutions that wouldn't have been developed otherwise. And he's not talking about only technological innovations, but rather, breakthrough approaches that impact service industries as well.

## The Role of the Consensus Builder

At this point it becomes clear that the innovator/champion needs to be a very special player: King Solomon, visionary, quarterback, father confessor, catalyst, and master consensus builder all rolled into one. In other words, someone with extraordinary people *and* communications skills.

Renowned psychologist Michael Kirton developed a profiling tool used to measure problem-solving styles, the Kirton Adaptive Innovation Inventory (KAI). Take a look at his general characteristics of Innovators:[*]

- Ingenious, original, independent, unconventional
- Challenges problem definition
- Does things differently
- Discovers problems and avenues for their solutions
- Manipulates problems by questioning existing assumptions
- Is a catalyst to unsettled groups, despite their consensual views
- Is capable of routine work for periods of short duration and is quick to delegate routine tasks
- Quickly takes control in unstructured situations

How do you fare?
Now let's examine his list of characteristics of adaptors:

- Efficient, thorough, methodical, organized, precise, reliable
- Accepts problem definition

---

[*] www.kaicentre.com.

- Does things better
- Concerned with resolving problems versus identifying them
- Seeks solutions in tried-and-true ways
- Reduces problems by improvement and enhanced efficiency, while aiming at continuity and stability
- Impervious to boredom, maintains high accuracy in long spells of detail work
- Takes authority within given structures

These are bundles of attributes, and—people being people—not everyone is all innovator or all adaptor. Innovation champions can have a variety of profiles, across a wide range, and their ideas and style of interaction are closely related and play a role in how effectively they can act as a true agent for change within an organization.

In "The Future of Survival of Corporate Innovation: Centers, Processes and Champions," authors Jack Hipple, David Hardy, Steve Wilson, and James Michalski studied corporate innovation centers and innovation champions.[*] Why, they asked, do innovation programs fail? What they found speaks to the importance of the innovation champion in democratizing the process, building consensus for the program throughout the organization, and making multiple champions.

According to this particular report, the "biggest barrier to success in these programs" was the tight focus on R&D and an exclusion of input from sales and marketing functions and the fact that the programs were funded at the expense of existing business technology budgets. Thus, the

[*] http://pubs.acs.org/subscribe/archive/ci/31/i11/html/11hipple.html.

door to a subtle but insidious form of sabotage was opened, and sales and marketing were reticent about participating or getting their fingerprints on the new effort.

The authors, in fact, suggest that "innovation centers" in the traditional sense, may not be the right model for today's organization. Innovate or die, to be sure. But be aware of the new ways to seed, cultivate, and harvest this innovation. These are the keys to success, according to this report. Sponsorship of the effort, among all the corporate elites, has to be wide.

Next, all functions need to become involved. Sales, marketing, finance, and manufacturing all need to be heard—and it's up to the innovation champion to ensure that this takes place.

In addition, diversity of experience and knowledge is critical, the authors say, echoing the words of Johnson & Johnson's Dr. Weisman.

When it's all clicking, employees willingly volunteer to work on even the riskiest new ventures. Employees offer stunning new business plans and product ideas, unsolicited. Ideas come in, over the transom, from unexpected places. People are sharing ideas, doing informal brainstorming at lunch or after work—groups that include designers, engineers, marketers—all living and breathing the project, with mutual respect and ready assistance. Customers ask to get in on the excitement and comment on your organization's ability to anticipate future product needs.

## The Path of an Innovation Champion

I asked Nic Hunt, Director of Innovation for an international manufacturing corporation, for a recap of how it all works, of how a culture of innovation is formed; the process driven by an innovation champion, who defeats the devil's advocates, is a true agent for change who democratizes the process and creates innovation acolytes throughout the organization. Nic takes a three-phase approach:

1. Define the desired culture.
2. Establish the foundations.
3. Engineer sustainability.

"The innovation culture," Hunt says, "once started, creates the passion that begets success, but this culture requires steady nurturing to keep it healthy and vibrant enough to evolve productively for the enterprise."

### Define the Desired Culture

Overall, defining the desired culture helps the organization understand the look and feel of innovative behavior, how to work together to achieve it, and, of course, how to share in the success it will bring. The importance of culture cannot be underestimated. Culture can enable or kill innovation.

This is a complex process that requires innovation champions to truly take the time to embed and to encourage trust and belief in the effort. It's all about behavior and walking the talk from the top down, rather than budgets and "throwing money at innovation."

To define the culture, you must:

- Quantify the magnitude of the goal, which, in turn, helps to identify and justify the resources that will be allocated. For example: "one new product per year" or "$25 million in new product sales in the next fiscal year."
- Define what innovation means in your organization. Draft the type of involvement, look, and feel that is expected.

- Identify the champions and key stakeholders you'll need to bring on board, including the key players of the community (technical, marketing, sales, etc.).
- Highlight examples of core innovations or innovators as beacons for the community and business at large. Initially, these may not even be from within the company.
- Decide how individuals will be recognized for delivering these examples.
- Audit this scenario against the existing culture to identify areas that require additional focus and pockets of excellence that already exist, as well as current business practices within your firm that may inadvertently be stifling innovation efforts.

### Establish the Foundations

Defining the desired culture, Nic explains, enables the innovation champion to deliver the culture change vision to the business. Establishing the foundation involves a range of strategies ranging from formal top-down approaches to user-managed tactics:

- *Start at the top.* The business leader must know, value, and own the innovation vision for the business. A key part of his or her role is to promote, endorse, and reinforce the commitment to innovation. ·
- *Create an identity or brand for innovation, in terms of something the business engages with.* This innovation brand, then, becomes the overarching theme for programs and initiatives created over time.
- *Within the vision, identify where structures are needed to frame an innovator's activities.* Examples

might include monthly innovation days, funds to recognize innovative brainstorming, an idea recognition process, or even off-campus team activities.

- *Identify when activities within these are likely to reach critical points.* Routinely publicize who owns them, who influences them, and how their success impacts the business strategy.
- *Formally establish communications channels reaching across the business.* Use multiple methods to create variety and reach the widest audience. Examples include employee newsletters, CEO webcasts, or even a notice board in a hallway corridor or common space such as a lunchroom.
- *Establish appropriate metrics to enable the success to be measured.* This helps build momentum and makes successes more tangible. Examples include *leading measures* such as measurement of new ideas collected and the value of the idea funding awarded over a period of time. *Lagging metrics* include the amount of money saved through innovative ideas, the number of customers delighted with new solutions or the monetary amount of sales attributable to new products;
- *Build a structured communications calendar to capture and share the successes.* Communication of "wins" helps build team morale and support for the innovation program. Surprisingly, telling the troops about "good news" is a step forgotten by team leaders, despite being far easier than the actual achievement.
- *Establish the framework for leadership involvement in innovation and forward schedules to ensure that this involvement actually happens.* Quarterly idea

reviews and monthly development meetings both work effectively.

- *Encourage organic cultural growth.* In smaller businesses, these "water cooler moments" typically occur unmanaged. However, in larger organizations, such tactics as bulletin boards, blogs, email directories, and other relationship tools help spur network building among people with mutual interests. Sharing information that helps individuals overcome challenges also demonstrates the size and value of being part of the innovation community. Connecting people is complex in larger organizations; there are many languages, legacy systems, and procedures set in place. Virtual communities that cut across business units require their own culture changes and management stewardship, and this is a truly worthwhile effort.

## Open Innovation: *Find the Balance*

Time to discuss *open innovation*, one of the hottest topics in business management today, in light of how it can accelerate the rewards from innovation.

Open innovation, in a sense, can be thought of as "innovation by partnership." The innovating small- or midsized company generates a game-changing product, technology, method, or design and works with a larger company to bring the dream to the marketplace. The innovating *larger* company, as part of its ongoing growth strategy, seeks access to externally developed intellectual property (IP).

Much has been written about open innovation, and, clearly, it is a process that can accelerate and stimulate opportunities for both the smaller and larger company. In my opinion, the biggest challenge is to conduct open innovation in a manner that promotes trust and respect. Often, the inventor or small business that approaches the large multinational with a brilliant concept gets manhandled and told, basically, "our way or the highway."

Open innovation agreements often demand ownership of the IP by the large multinational, in exchange for their investment, and taking on marketing and distribution. I have found that many investors and small business owners do not have the leverage or the means to counter what can be perceived as a significant inequality. In years past, open innovation activity is driven by the large companies, which have much to gain—especially if they own the IP.

It takes courage, leverage, and toughness to create a balanced open innovation relationship. It is not unusual for large multinationals to patent IP while you are sharing and developing, or even reengineering, to launch outside of the existing, submitted IP. In a balanced relationship, the IP or technology of the inventors or small businesses should remain theirs. These are the specialists in key areas and, in my opinion, should own what they have developed and are focused on.

A key question, however, is what happens when two technologies "meet" to create a new IP? For instance, imagine a dispenser company that develops a unique, patented technology with clear-cut consumer benefits. Should the marketer own the IP in its entirety?

So does open innovation provide opportunity, or does it unnecessarily tie up the inventor's IP and choke growth potential?

I'll admit I'm an entrepreneurial type and I have my opinions. In the interest of balanced reporting, we interviewed Chris Thoen, the brilliant Managing Director–Open Innovation Office (Connect + Develop), Procter & Gamble Company. P&G is the New York Yankees of packaged goods. According to company literature, "Three billion times a day, P&G brands touch the lives

(continued)

(*continued*)

of people around the world." The company has one of the most robust portfolios of trusted, quality, and, yes, innovative brands, including such iconic names as Pampers, Tide, Gillette, Dawn, Pringles, Iams, Crest, Braun, and Duracell.

The first thing we asked Thoen was how they go about searching for IP. He explained how the company has both reactive and proactive ways to address open innovation.

On the reactive side, he first directed us to www.pgconnect develop.com. This is a must-visit site. Clearly, the company has an unrelenting focus on innovation and wants to partner with the world's finest innovators. "We believe in win-win deals and in building relationships," the home page states. "Could your innovation be the next game-changing deal?" On this site, one can learn more about the Connect + Develop program, submit innovations, actually peruse current P&G IP needs, and much more—one-stop shopping for those seeking open innovation opportunities. Every business unit is reviewing submissions that came through the web site. And, yes, there are versions in Japanese and Chinese as well. In only two-plus years, the program has yielded 7,500 submissions. The assessment process, he said, takes four to five weeks.

"Where can we find innovators? That's the question we ask ourselves," Thoen said. "It could be internally. And, at the same time, we've looked at what we need to achieve and have realized that we need more creative ideas than we can generate ourselves. We search for creative ecosystems outside our walls and look for that special 'connection,'" he said. "Our program helps us manage contacts, as we do more innovating 'outside.'"

The real key to success for the Connect + Develop program is "to know what you need," he said. Too generalized a definition yields inferior results—"too wooly" is how Thoen puts it. The result? P&G developed a comprehensive "needs brief" form, with the title ("New delivery approaches or new forms for existing colorants that provide more vibrant, long-lasting colors"), types (materials, technology), categories, description ("longer lasting color for lip color, mascara, and facial makeup . . . "), a PDF for the complete needs brief file, and date of need.

The following screen capture details the complete technical problem, including background, objectives, possible approaches, constraints, potential partner capabilities and even criteria for success:

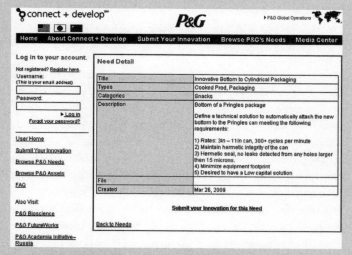

*Source:* Procter & Gamble (www.pgconnectdevelop.com/pg connection-portal/ctx/noauth/0_0_1_4_83_4_15.do).

These are nonconfidential submissions, Thoen explained. "Innovators must have their IP in place before they submit," he said. "This gives them protection and gives us valuable assurances as well. IP helps us create a competitive advantage."

"The idea," he said, "is to create a positive experience when working with P&G."

Proactively, P&G has an elite cadre of 70 technology entrepreneurs, placed around the world in Connect + Develop hubs.

*(continued)*

*(continued)*

"Their sole mission is to tap into local universities, companies, and venture capital firms and meet with inventors," Thoen said. "They search for possibilities, setting up a 'network of networks,' connecting the dots and forging relationships."

"This is their day job, and they possess a singular set of skills," he said. "We recruit strong technologists, to weed-and-feed ideas. And they also have the soft skills that enable them to make connections that are not readily apparent to most people. Our technology entrepreneurs love music, art, literature, and superb people skills."

Is it working? Topical antimicrobial specialists Syntopix Group signed a joint technology development agreement, based on an unsolicited proposal through the Connect + Develop web site. Then there's a small French company with a new peptide technology that wound up being a key component in the blockbuster product, Olay Regenerist, a $2 billion brand. A candle company's expertise helped the Febreze brand bring Febreze candles to the marketplace. A Japanese firm partnered with P&G to deliver the Oral-B Pulsonic Toothbrush, which was in-market less than a year after the first meeting. Like Pringles Stix? This was a result of a Japanese food company–P&G partnership, which brought the product to North America.

The list is endless. . . .

### Engineer Sustainability

In this phase, we create the tools that nurture the innovation culture over time. The process requires innovation management to actively drive these elements. Once developed, the system will yield successes that need to be shared quickly and effectively, in order to further the program's vitality and efficacy.

To engineer sustainability, you must:

- *Develop imagery and symbols to help bring the program to life.* Include internal innovation awards, patent recognition badges, and innovator lunches.
- *Share success stories that provide examples of great teamwork and superior outcomes.* They should be captured in a format that can be circulated, digested, and appreciated organization-wide.
- *Create regular activities that help build a sense of purpose.* This includes news updates, monthly meetings, and weekly, themed brainstorming sessions.
- *Create structure for organizational contributors to the innovation effort.* Examples include a method for evaluation of ideas, a process for allowing individual ideators access to designer time, and so on.
- *Identify and establish where key positions need to be created or structures changed to enable organic growth of innovation.* Examples might include a knowledgeable manager, additional internal communications—even creation of a design studio.
- *Cultivate the innovation power structure to identify those highly respected organizational leaders that are positioned as stewards who promote the culture.* These may not necessarily be the most senior people—advocacy from long-serving, proven professionals is extremely powerful for the majority of the organizational community.

Spread the excitement of the new innovation program. It works. All sorts of employees and business partners have wonderful ideas and are eager to participate in the process and make their unique voices heard.

## The Innovation Payoff: A Quick, Real-Life Story

To that last point, I am reminded of my most recent conversation with Frank Feraco. Frank was president of Sterling Plumbing Group and, later, an executive vice president at Kohler Company, and is currently managing partner, Great Lakes Equity Partners. He has been a mentor and friend through much of my professional career. I asked him about building a culture of innovation and how good things happen from this effort. And, in typical Feraco fashion, he responded with a fabulous story:

> It's 1981 and I'm at Emerson Electric. The company bought SKIL Powertool, a good company that was underperforming. *We had to fix it!*
>
> I show up, we start a listening process, we see what we have. We tell them, "There are no dumb ideas." We encourage ideas. And, truly, they have a great brand. Distributors love them. But no planning, nothing. The owners of the business didn't see a need for new product development. They thought they could survive forever on their brand's strength. Meantime, they were up against Mikita, Bosch, and Black & Decker. I told management, "Hang on, we'll turn this around."
>
> One day soon afterward, an engineer, Alex Gowran, comes into my office. He says, "I have this new product, been working on it for 15 years, but nobody's been interested." He takes out a cylindrical tool, with a screwdriver tip. I thought, "We could fine-tune the technology of the electric motor, give it enough torque to turn the screw. And we could tinker with the design, but this is something: the first cordless, electric screwdriver, for the consumer."

Retail hardware stores would eat this up, I just know it. We tested prototypes, it was doable, all right. But it wasn't patentable, so we had one shot to launch it, and launch it right. We had no cash and we needed about $3 million for television commercials, to get it done in time to market for Christmas gift giving, to prime the market for Black Friday. We needed a champion. I get a meeting with the chairman of Emerson, the parent company, and, with marketing, we made our pitch for the money. He accepted the proposal, with one caveat: "Go get it," he says, "but if you fail to deliver, someone has to pay!" Most likely, me.

Bottom line, we win Product of the Year. The competition was scooped for Christmas. Distributors are clamoring for product. Harvard Business School does a case study on our success. It leads to five separate new products, each one a winner. Huge pretax margins. A halo for SKIL. Ultimately, the company is sold to Bosch for a sum well beyond anyone's expectations. A classic success story of how innovation, plus operating excellence, equals great value.

Become an agent for change. Beat the devil's advocates. It can pay off, big time.

## Think About

- What was your organization's last showstopper?
- Was it developed internally or via open innovation?
- How productive are your ideation sessions?
- On a scale from 1 to 10, with 1 being poor and 10 being superb, how would you rate the people and communications skills of your organization's innovation champion?

# CHAPTER 5

# Innovation in the Time of Multinational Teams

Whatis the nature of the creative type? How can they be best motivated? And how, in our global world, can creatives from various geographic regions, with hugely different cultural points of orientation, be managed in a way that brings out their best and results in sustainable innovation?

In this chapter, I examine the nature of the creative mind-set and discuss the care and feeding of creatives. Then, I delve into what it takes to be a global team leader, examine team building techniques, and look at how various cultures operate in meetings and in team environments.

## The Care and Feeding of Creatives

Just curious: What is *your* opinion of creative individuals? How are they perceived within your organization?

I am reminded of a friend who once worked at a large public relations agency in New York City. His 22nd-floor office window faced south, where he saw the green expanse of Bryant Park and, less than 10 blocks away, the majestic Empire State Building.

One day, this friend struggled with a "big idea" for a new business proposal that represented a significant amount of incremental billings for his agency. He had been in his office grappling with the problem and was on the brink of the million-dollar solution. But he just wasn't quite there yet. He put down his yellow legal pad and pencil, turned his seat around so as to face the wide window, put his feet up on the radiator, and stared vacantly at the New York streetscape before him.

Just then, he caught sight of his boss's reflection in his office window. "Oh," said the boss, cynically, "busy as a bee, huh?"

What are highly charged creative people like? I've known many. Sometimes they might *seem* as if they are "spacing out," like my New York friend in the story. Sometimes they are uncommunicative—verbally, that is. You'd think you were talking to a sulking adolescent. Sometimes they act out. They resist when they feel restricted by what they consider "too much process" or confining corporate culture.

Some have limited social skills and prefer to work alone, in a denlike environment of their own creation. Back in the day when smoking in one's office was not an offense punishable by death, I remember one particular member of my creative team who would stay in her office, door closed, smoking furiously as she worked out business problems. We'd wonder, *is she okay in there? Is she alive?* Then, we'd hear her heavy smoker's cough. *Well, she's still alive*, we'd think.

And always, the next morning, a brilliant treatise with the solution to the vexing problem would be waiting for me on my desk.

They need their space, these creative folks. The trick, I've found over the years, is to find the right ones, wind them up, let them go, and stay out of their way.

At meetings, you'll find that your true creative types will be the ones to ask the most challenging, interesting questions, probing at the weak underbelly of a solution.

"What if . . . ?" their questions will begin. And they'll keep probing, making some people a bit uncomfortable. It'll be done not out of malice, but out of intellectual curiosity and passion and the sheer joy—the thrill—of getting to the heart of the thorniest, knotted shoelace of a problem.

And you, wise and successful manager that you no doubt are, will cock your head and nod and realize the worth to the organization of this type of individual. And then you'll smile because you know that this is the creativity that leads to innovation that, in turn, results in rewarding and profitable solutions.

But what happens when this type of creative personality is told "no"—for any reason? What happens when their manager prefers to stick to a certain procedure? Many times, it's thunder, drama, push-back, a "spirited debate." There is an art to telling a creative individual "no." There is a trick to providing "feedback."

For the first part, keep the restraints off during ideation sessions. The practical, real-world filters can always be put back later in the process. I've been in ideation sessions where the facilitator will place a coffee can in the middle of the conference room table. Attendees are required to put cash in the can if they channel their inner Dilbert and respond to ideas with any of the following statements:

"That'll never work."

"We tried that last year and . . . "

"But we don't have the budget for that . . . "

"It's impossible to fabricate . . . "

The money went toward pizzas, as invariably that group would work very late and would call for deliveries. And the more important the session, the higher their penalty for ideation kill.

Vin Raby, Vice President, Global Product Development, Rexam Personal Care Division, understands the interplay of skills between product innovation, development, and management. Exhibit 5.1 explains the qualities necessary to succeed at each, and the relationship of each group to the other. Clearly, there is convergence in the middle. Product management must have more demonstrable, specific marketplace expertise, with a moderate amount of both creativity and engineering know-how.

Product development people skew toward having the finest grasp of engineering precision, and relatively less ability on the "creativity" side of the scale. The product innovation folks, however, are the creativity-oriented group, and it's important for management to be aware of, understand, and have respect for each group's strengths. Further, management expectations about each group's respective roles and responsibilities need to be calibrated along these lines.

Managing the creative individuals in your organization can be a joy or a curse, depending on your particular view,

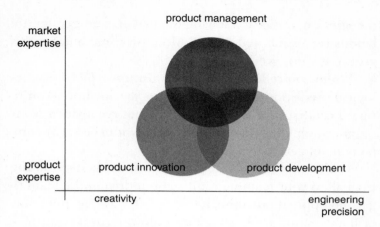

**Exhibit 5.1    Interplay of Skills**
*Source:* Vin Raby.

which is why I asked that question at the start of this chapter.

In my experience, the central issue is to keep one's own ego out of the process. And I have to admit that this is hard, for me as well as many professionals I know, because we are successful, strong-willed, practical, and knowledgeable individuals. In my heart of hearts, I often feel I know what's right, what's wrong, what works, and what doesn't.

The members of your creative team march to the beat of a different drum. They come in late, or when they're in on time, they may not really get started until late in the day. But then, their lights will be on until two in the morning.

## For Creative People, It's about More than Money

Money isn't necessarily the be-all and end-all in terms of their motivation. For many creatives, a key driver is recognition, notice for solving the problem and congratulations for "a job well done." Money is great but, for this group, it's not everything.

When you're leading a team with this type of psychological predisposition, it's not about *you* anymore. You're now a catalyst in a process. Where does creativity in your organization come from? Your *team*. Not necessarily company management.

You're the basketball point guard, deftly distributing the ball to your teammates. It's about driving the team to get the optimal outcome, a team of creative, iconoclastic, brilliant—and, true, sometimes downright eccentric—men and women who take pride in their ability and don't like (and, more importantly, don't work at their best with) shackles on their synapses.

Let your creatives feel safe to fail. Give them space to do their thing, and let the entire team be heard. Remember, too, that the "entire team" is not necessarily your R&D department—open it up. And, as you do so, remember that your most creative "players" may be willful, prideful, determined, passionate—not a group of sheep, by any means. They have to feel safe and empowered to do their best work.

However, management must simultaneously take pains to ensure that others within the organization do not feel marginalized or harbor a grudge toward those "creatives" for whom the rules can seemingly bend at will.

Willful, indeed. I am reminded of the famous 3M story that has become part of U.S. business culture folklore. It is the tale of how 3M's CEO at the time, ordered a staffer to quit a project, since it was thought that it was bound to fail. The employee ignored the edict and kept on, ultimately inventing the breakthrough product—masking tape—and setting the stage for that iconic 3M product, Scotch tape.

There are, today, companies where it is expected for certain group—researchers, scientists, and so on—to spend a certain percentage of their time on discretionary projects. Work of their own choosing, with autonomy, much like the original Lockheed Martin skunk works.

Why encourage something that some might think of as "a complete waste of time"? Creativity and "output" are linked. I apologize for continuing the basketball analogy, but the more "shots" at the basket your creative team takes, the better the chance that the ball will go through the hoop. The more they'll score. Of course, the more shots they take, the more shots they'll *miss*, too. Which is why it is critical for creatives to feel safe to fail.

Experts in human resources and leaders of creative individuals understand the many ways in which management can extinguish the creative flame. It's actually quite easy. Otherwise savvy business executives do it all the time, sometimes on purpose, but mostly inadvertently. Here's how it's done:

- Dominate the creative process and alienate the team players.
- Ignore or override input from the group.
- Refute recommendations by saying, "That won't work because . . . "
- Don't keep track of meeting decisions and next steps.
- Don't schedule ideation sessions or other communication "rituals."
- Fail to recognize creatives' contributions.

However, there are many ways for managers to encourage creativity among innovation team members. Again, the key is for managers to keep their egos out of the way. Let go. Delegate responsibility and encourage ownership. At the same time, it's equally important to recognize achievements—and in the right way.

Here's yet another tip, from Kevin Hummel, PhD, president and founder of Lighthouse Consulting Group (www.lighthouseconsultinggroup.com). This expert in industrial and organizational psychology relates this technique, mastered by his mentor, Marshall Goldsmith. Hummel explains the dynamic tension that results from giving "feedback." It's uncomfortable for the manager, and it's equally unsettling for the employee. "Critical feedback makes you feel as if you're being judged—because you are," Hummel said in my recent interview with him. "Instead, try providing 'feed-forward.' Work with the person to mutually agree upon targets for improvement."

This, he explained, helps take the emotion out of the situation and, instead, create a coaching culture that assures more positive outcomes. "For example, rather than upbraiding the team—'why aren't we more creative?'—provide the feed-forward 'what do we need to be doing to drive innovation?' Develop a list, and have team members pick an item and sign up for it." Ah yes: accountability. "This is an approach used by Fortune 50 companies, smaller companies, nonprofits—it works."

Let's recap tips regarding the "care and feeding of creatives" before we place an overlay of how global leaders can effectively marshal their international network of creatives and build an international team.

When building a team of creative individuals, remember to:

- Select people with "the right stuff"—from across disciplines, driven, proud, unafraid to reach for the stars.

- Use your motivational skills by creating clear and unwavering deadline pressure, while reinforcing and praising their incremental progress and fostering a sense of "team spirit." Sure, the assignment is mission critical, it's tense, it's needed. But it should also be fun, a challenge. Leave them to push themselves to heights you never imagined was possible.

- Reward success and praise failure—create an environment where mistakes are tolerated, absent of punitive measures. Remember that creative success is a ratio, and you want to encourage your players to take their shots. The more shots taken, the more points will be scored. If you're bound and determined to punish "someone" for a failure of innovation, punish those who slough off their assignment and can't/won't even "take the shot." Fire people who don't flop enough, some might say. That's rather harsh, in my opinion, but you get the point.

- Let your A-team work to their potential—select players who are a bit iconoclastic, who push the envelope a bit. Let their passion have free rein.

- Make selective use of your veto power—when a creative person is hot on the trail of an idea, in full pursuit of the prize, temper your ability and authority to pull the plug on the project and let him or her defend the project's ability to create incremental revenue to the fullest.

- Initially filter idea killers—especially in ideation sessions, as these can always be added back into the equation once the creative session results are reviewed. Think about this: The process of fostering creativity will initially result in ideas that are practical, and some that are very impractical. It's the nature of the process.

- Help creatives transition concepts to workable ideas by adding back the structure, as necessary, to help visualize the idea in the context of market needs, budget requirements, and manufacturability. Just keep the funnel open as wide as possible in the initial phase of the process. Many creative individuals have a wonderful ability to see "the big picture" from the outset.

- Provide regular and fair feedback, and keep the lines of communication open (remembering that communication is a two-way street). Constructive feedback and guidance is not the same as saying, *"Wrong!"* Respect for the risk takers can be difficult for you to show, but is invaluable in its impact on *esprit de corps*.

- Think long and hard about mixing your creatives with customers in the same ideation session in the hope of spurring new heights of creativity. As I said earlier, yes, it can work. Depends on the customer. But remember: Customers, like (unfortunately) some managers, can be quick to criticize all but the most practical, logical solutions. They are money people. They are not invested in the success of an internal ideation session or in the personal feelings and temperament of your creative team. Trust me on this: I have seen the most creative people at advertising agencies clam up tight when a client was introduced to participate in a brainstorming session. The chemistry changes, the fear of failure raises its ugly head, and the whole enterprise shuts down. Customer input is invaluable to the ideation process. Just don't mix your customer with your internal idea guys and gals at the same meeting without a whole lot of thought beforehand.

## Babel, Babble, and the Global Team Leader

Working with the creative temperament can be challenging and rewarding, like a good game of chess. Factor in the challenge of managing international teams, and it becomes a bit like playing *three-dimensional* chess.

Within any one country, we can safely say that everyone's a bit different. Then, from country to country, we behave differently, think differently, respond to team building differently. It becomes critical for global team leaders to be aware of, understand, and respect these cultural differences.

Culture is the context within which we live and conduct business. And innovate. As global team leader, it's imperative to experience, firsthand, the environment of each major group in the team, in order to understand the nuances that will color every statement, every group session.

Often, cross-cultural groups hold their meetings in English. But are you all *thinking in English?* Are you all *equally proficient in English?*

What about interpersonal relationships? Cultural differences, country to country, impact what behaviors are acceptable, considered gauche, confrontational, silly, or disrespectful. No doubt you already are aware that some numbers are lucky, some unlucky, depending on the culture. This is merely the tip of the iceberg. Facial expressions, hand gestures, typical business attire—these all vary with the culture.

What is the prevailing religion of the country? What is the nature of the family structure? What about political orientation? The global team leader needs to be aware of sensitivities and predispositions. And that's still not all of it.

What about humor? What's funny in one country can be perceived as extremely gauche, even downright insulting, in another.

Is the country's communication style explicit or implicit? In the United States, for example, there is an explicit communication style. It is assumed that the listener has no prior awareness of the back-story on any particular issue and, as a matter of course, the communicator fills in the blanks. To the explicit communicator, this makes sense. To the implicit listener, who instinctively prefers to "connect the dots" and build awareness through inference—and who is capable of quickly getting "it"—this approach sounds like "overkill."

In Japan, however, it is typically assumed that the listener is aware of the back-story and therefore (and understandably, given that context) provides much less information. To the implicit communicator, this makes perfect sense. To the explicit listener, this approach sounds "vague."

## Team Building, One Step at a Time

Congratulations, global team leader. You are your group's de facto United Nations. Not only are you charged with keeping your ego out of the way and creating an environment that nurtures creativity and accepts failure as part of the price of the process, but you are the traffic cop, Supreme Court, and central contact point for creative personalities *from countries around the world!*

At this point, it might be understandable if you resigned this particular role and decided to stick to your "day job." It would be difficult enough managing a creative team in either the United States or Brazil or France. But a multicultural team? Mon dieu!

I'm here to say that it can be done. It's not easy, but it can be done. You just have to take it step by step. Remember the value of opening the innovation team to those across divisions and across disciplines, and to those of various backgrounds. Now we're adding other textures, from various countries. The outcome will be all the richer for it.

Remember to always retain your sensitivity to the feelings of others from different cultures. There is no "right way" to conduct business, and no "wrong way," either. There sure are different ways, though.

For starters, here is a sampling of business-situation topics that I frequently ponder. These are merely the first course in our review of how to build international teams of creatives in the pursuit of sustainable innovation:

- *Hierarchy protocol.* Hierarchy in some countries defers to age, while in others, to the highest-ranking group member. Some defer to masculine gender.
- *Time.* I hear a slow exhale of breath as you read this, muttering, "Why are they *sooo slow?*" Or "Why are they *in such a rush?*" Building relationships with new members of the group is critical. Take time to establish rapport, rather than rushing to "the task

at hand," as is typically done in the United States. Remember that attitudes toward time and work vary widely.

- *Attire.* In face-to-face meetings, your choice of attire is a signal of respect to others in the group. Be aware of regional differences, and err on the side of conservative or middle-of-the-road attire.

- *The business card ritual.* As with other elements in the cross-cultural equation, the exchange of business cards should be approached with "respect" for the other party of paramount importance. Offer your card once you are introduced to a new team member. Those from the Pacific Rim are used to receiving cards offered with two hands, right side up for immediate reading. Upon receiving a card from an Asian, regard it carefully and place it with care in your card case.

- *Personal space.* Some cultures are "touch-y." Some get very close during conversation. Here in the United States, people value their personal space. It's important to be aware of, and respect, regional differences.

- *Formality.* Surprising as it may be to many North Americans, not everyone in the world calls people by their first name at first meeting. The informality of those in the United States is not shared by those in every country, where first name usage is for family and long-time friends. To be safe, refer to new introductions with professional title and last name, until invited to do otherwise.

- *The handshake.* As a corollary to formality, remember, too, that not everyone in the world shares the American penchant for a firm, quick handshake, smile, and direct eye contact. The firmness of the handshake varies country to country (Japanese, light; German, firm; Middle Eastern, continuous through the greeting, etc.).

## Viva la Difference!

You are armed with an understanding of what makes creative individuals tick. You understand what motivates and demotivates them. You see the value of bringing together team members from different backgrounds and from different countries, and see the importance of respecting basic cultural differences you might encounter in the workplace.

"Specifics!" you shout. "Give me specifics!" You may have worked with someone from France at some point, or maybe had an intern from China in your office one summer. But what can you expect when you create a Dirty Dozen innovation team from the Americas, Europe, the Pacific Rim?

As with any group, generalizing can be counter-productive. Everyone is different, we are told from the time we enter preschool. We are all unique individuals. Yet in my experience with multinational teams of professionals, I have found certain commonalities among people from different countries, in terms of how they:

- React in a meeting environment
- Approach the concept of "teamwork"
- Communicate with others

Speaking only for myself, here is what I found over three decades of professional experience.

## United States: Informal, Enthusiastic, Embraces Team Play, In Your Face, Hates to Waste Time

From preschool on, American children are encouraged to form teams to solve problems and participate in a variety of activities, from sports to the arts. The commitment to the group is considered a virtue, and team members learn quickly that the group's achievement is the primary objective. Participants are earnest, guileless.

Teams flourish, accomplish goals, and are disbanded. New teams are formed, and again the needs of the individual are subsumed by the common purpose. This fluidity—from group formation to disbanding to reformation—is de rigueur to those in the States. The transitory nature of group formation is akin to a wide range of elements in the U.S. culture.

How do Americans act in meetings? Some of the words that come to mind are "in your face," "aggressive," "confrontational." The constant level of debate or push-back can be offputting to the global team leader, and it will be important for him or her to make sure the Americans don't run roughshod over those from regions where direct confrontation is just not done. The key thing to remind other team members is that this aggression is not personal (well, most of the time, anyway!). It's simply the way it's done here, where the clock is king and time is money. *No time for dickering, let's get right to it*—that's a common approach in the United States.

Presentations are a big part of the meeting scene here, and great care is taken to create visually impressive, technically superior "decks." Teammates rehearse their presentations for impactful delivery, as well as to ensure they do not run over their time allotment at the meeting. That would be a no-no.

As for communication style, many Americans come off just plain rude. What's considered courteous, discreet, or civil in some lands is perceived as "simply a big waste of time" by many in the States. It's not hostility. It's just, well, "direct." Once something is agreed to at a meeting, it gets done.

And speaking of direct, many Americans discuss private matters—and ask about private matters—as a matter of course and in an intrusive, overt way that can make others blanch.

### France: Competitive, "Day-Job" Oriented, Heavily Formatted and Hierarchical Meetings, Sophisticated Use of and Appreciation for Language and Communication Skills

Given the competitive nature of the education system in France, team play is not always the first priority among youngsters, a trait that continues into the adult, professional years. This can limit the ability of the employee to transfer loyalties from the so-called "day job" to the innovation team.

In meeting situations, "the boss is the boss," and the purpose of the meeting is frequently to merely recap, or communicate, decisions that were made previously. Yes, lots of things get discussed and are agreed upon prior to the actual meeting. And things agreed upon at the actual meeting, for execution, may just not happen and will be raised for discussion months later.

The agenda is set, and the participants have their roles. The boss is rarely contradicted. Therefore, a key to success is working the backchannels in advance of the meeting, to sway consensus and build support for a particular idea or position. Time and punctuality is less of a driver than in some cultures. Team members will saunter into international meetings late, without apology. A fixation on the clock is the other guy's problem.

In terms of communication, French executives are quite skillful and have great respect for precision of language and sophisticated constructions. There is a passion for finding the perfect expression or word, and parsing the language can be what it's all about.

Like Americans, French communication in peer-to-peer situations can be overt or perceived as extremely confrontational to those from other cultures.

### Brazil: Relationship Building Heightens Results, Hierarchy-Oriented, Relatively Informal Meeting Style, Direct Eye Contact, Bold Body Language, Passionate Verbal Communication

Teams in Brazil take time to develop but, once forged, can be very powerful. A key is to take time to build a comfort level with your Brazilian team members and establish a personal bond.

Team members prefer to know their precise roles and the details of the chain of command, in my experience. Without such a hierarchy in place, the global team leader can expect to be on the receiving end of even smaller problems or questions. Interteam communication on such matters should not be a given.

Meetings, at first, might seem a little stiff, but once relationships are formed and a comfort level built, an informal style is quickly introduced. This comfort level is built around layers and layers of personal discussion, which frequently prefaces the actual meeting. It is critical to let this discussion play out fully and to not cut it short, as it creates the social glue that binds you and the team members.

Time issues and punctuality are less of an absolute than in some Anglo or Asian cultures. Expect meetings to start late and to meander through the agenda. All topics will be addressed but not necessarily in linear progression. Being, and appearing to be, relaxed has great currency.

In terms of communication and language, there are a few key points regarding Brazil. Many executives here speak excellent English, but it's not universal. Do not make the mistake of offering your high school Spanish in an attempt to converse. While well intentioned, Brazilians are proud of their language and country and will correct your Spanish with the right Portuguese phrase.

Expect passionate explanations enhanced by great physicality.

### China: Consensus Oriented, Bias against Unilateral Action, Demonstrates and Expects Respect, Finds It Difficult to Say "No"

Chinese culture is consensus driven, which leads to a team orientation; the individual needs are sublimated for the good of the group. In terms of creating an environment where sustainable innovation will flourish, it is important for the global team leader to be aware of the fact that the Chinese team member may be reticent about publicly stating bold viewpoints or countering someone's argument in public. To stand out from the crowd is a negative and generally is not done, meaning it will be up to the leader to draw the best ideas out of this team member, perhaps offline and out of the team meeting spotlight, which is to be avoided at all costs.

An important note for first meetings: The business card *is* the executive, and the exchange of cards requires respect and careful attention to protocol. The card is held in both hands and proffered right side up. Upon receiving your team member's card, read it carefully and place it with dignity in a card case. A cursory look and placement in a shirt or jacket pocket is unacceptable. Further, you may find—at first meeting—that your new team member from China lowers his or her eyes rather than establishing direct eye contact. It is often considered impolite to look a guest directly in the eye, and customary to look down, out of respect.

Speaking of body language, the Chinese are not overt, a style that can be mistaken for "disinterest" or "unemotional" or "impassive." It is a cultural difference that must be recognized, understood, expected, and deciphered.

Decision making is generally not done by the conclusion of a meeting but, rather, afterwards, offline, in a series of mini-meetings, as consensus is built. It takes time to get to an agreement, and the matter is compounded by a reluctance to say "no." If a response is anything less than a resounding "yes!" it probably means "no."

## Aretha Was Right: It's All About R-E-S-P-E-C-T

Where does this sampling of cultural differences leave the global team leader?

It is incumbent upon the leader of the innovation team to remember that cultural influences play a key role in who we are and how we approach work and business as adults.

In a sense, we are hard-wired to behave according to the cultural cues of our early years, and this programming lasts a long time, even after we move to new countries and "acclimate." The "old ways" are still there, under the surface, directing psychic traffic.

So what's to be done? Realize that the differences exist, respect the differences, and understand that it's a two-way street. And always remember:

- An idea is an idea is an idea—no one person from a particular country has a lock on creativity.
- Imagine how your cultural style is being perceived from those in the group who hail from other lands.
- English may be a universal language, but it's important to remember that, with those who speak English as a second language, the degree of nuance and subtlety may vary widely.
- Communicate, communicate, and communicate some more.
- Hold regular information exchanges and get your team together in person, as often as possible.
- Keep your multinational team at ease by overtly encouraging mutual respect for all.

## Think About

- Do you consider managing creative people more of a curse or a blessing? Why?
- How would you rate the diversity of your team, in terms of function, geographic profile, gender, ethnicity, and so on? What can be improved?
- Have you experienced a culture clash recently? If so, how was it resolved?

# 6

# Patently Obvious

## THE CARE AND FEEDING OF YOUR INTELLECTUAL PROPERTY

Innovation helps your company "win" in many ways. One of the more easily monetized ways to win is by patenting your intellectual property (IP). Create a portfolio of patents and watch your company valuation climb.

Entrepreneurial types can, at times, have great ambivalence regarding the legal profession. At any informal gathering of business acquaintances, the talk invariably turns to the legal profession, at which point the jokes begin. An oldie but goodie:

**Question:** What do you call 20,000 lawyers at the bottom of the ocean?
**Answer:** A good start!

Now that I've gotten that out of my system, we can productively move on to the business at hand. Every high-performance businessperson has their share of frustration with their company's legal department or outside firm. However, in terms of building sustainable innovation, there is no getting around the fact that there are three legs on the stool:

1. Technology
2. Business acumen
3. Law

This is why one of the Robert's Rules of Innovation imperatives is *Idea Management*. The IP attorney is essential to the care and feeding—protection— of your idea(s). Patents are important tools for both offensive and defensive strategy. Therefore, in this chapter, I will provide an overview of IP topics, delve deeper into a discussion of IP 101, and then drill down to tackle the most frequently asked questions on the subject.

This information comes to you via three trusted attorneys from firms specializing in Intellectual Property (IP) and/or global trade law: Glenn Henneberger, partner at Hoffmann & Baron, LLP (www.hoffmannbaron.com); Gary S. Winer, patent attorney at Fleit Gibbons Gutman Bongini & Bianco PL (www.fggbb.com); and Rick Van Arnam, partner at Barnes Richardson and Colburn (www.barnesrichardson.com). I've worked with these attorneys, and their firms are first rate. In addition, the web sites referenced here are invaluable sources of information, as is the web site of the U.S. Patent and Trademark Office (www.uspto.gov), as well as www.patents.com and www.google.com/patents. I urge you to bookmark these URLs immediately.

## Intellectual Property: The Big Picture

Business growth and innovative products are dynamically interlinked. A headline in *BusinessWeek* magazine this year that announced "American Business Loses Ground in U.S. Patents" went on to state that U.S. companies accounted for fewer than half of the nearly 183,000 patents issued by the United States last year, down a percentage point from 2007.* Whether this correlates with the state of U.S. business is the stuff of a great conversation. Whatever your viewpoint, the reality is that innovation leads to business success and that this innovation needs to be managed and protected. And that is where the IP attorneys and their work with the USPTO come into play.

"It really is a three-legged stool," says attorney Gary Winer. "You can't only rely on marketing to carry the day, or business measures such as cost-cutting."

"Intellectual property law," he adds, "puts a fence, and often many fences, around your innovation to keep competitors at bay, so they can't copy, use, import, or sell it, either accidentally or through reverse engineering."

Legal protection is more important than ever in today's global marketplace, where competitors lie in wait around the world. Working with the right IP attorneys can help prevent your firm from stepping on another company's IP, keeping you out of harm's way in terms of costly (in terms of time and money) lawsuits. They can also help you protect your valuable trademarks and trade names against counterfeiting and other unauthorized uses. IP lawyers also assist in valuation of the firm's IP, so important during mergers, acquisitions, or when

---

*Tara Kalwarski, *BusinessWeek*, March 23–30, 2009.

seeking outside venture capital. Strong protection of IP gives investors that warm and fuzzy feeling that makes good things happen for your firm.

To recap, the IP firm actually procures the intellectual property protection for the client, enforces it, and handles the due diligence on IP valuation when it's time to purchase or license it, and much more.

What is the mind of the IP attorney like, relative to other types of lawyers you may have worked with in the past? It's an interesting hybrid mind-set.

They can be a bit geeky, in a very good way. It is a fairly "squeaky clean" profession. IP attorneys who are registered to practice before the Patent Office all have a technical background, with many having earned degrees in engineering. Their desire to be at the cutting edge of science drives many of them to IP law. "Many inventions developed in the lab are further refined and expanded upon during the process of preparing patent applications," says Glenn Henneberger, attorney at Hoffmann & Baron, LLP.

IP attorneys hold business degrees, as well. They're scientists who know what it takes to succeed in business and are also experts in the intricacies of patent law. They're very smart, very cool, and absolutely invaluable.

"It's really about having the knowledge and judgment and communications skills to be able to put ourselves in our clients' shoes, understand the business, and get our clients where they want to go, so that their IP is solidly protected," Winer says.

Adds Henneberger, "The ideal relationship is one of partnership and mutual respect. We have developed strong relationships with many of our clients and have helped them grow their businesses over the years."

Equating IP attorneys with "patents" is, I admit, an over-simplification. They handle patents, as well as trademarks, copyrights, unfair competition, trade secrets, false advertising, computer law, Internet law, technology licensing, and related litigation, and serve as expert witnesses.

In selecting your IP law firm, there are a variety of factors to consider. And, if you are reading this book, you quite likely have IP assets that need legal protection via a patent, trademark, or copyright. For those not currently working with a law firm, a great place to start is with references from associates in your various business groups, your general counsel or general practice law firm, your CPAs, or from mentions you might find in selected trade journals.

Visit the firm's web site and review the list of attorneys working with the firm, scanning for those with direct experience in your product or service arena. Are you comfortable that this firm has a focus on IP? Are the attorneys registered to practice before the USPTO? Do they have degrees in engineering and/or expertise in your specific industry? Do they handle only "the big guys," where litigation can dominate the activity, or do they also work with small and midsized firms? Is their area of specialization in one primary area (entertainment, financial products, machinery, nuclear processing)?

## Intellectual Property 101

Clearly, there is a lot to think about, in terms of understanding the importance of the IP protection process, and in selecting the right IP law firm for you. But the stakes get higher and higher as your sustainable innovation process gathers momentum and fabulous new ideas accelerate through your new product development (NPD) system.

Glenn Henneberger holds a degree in electrical engineering, is registered to practice before the USPTO, was a practicing electrical engineer, and is an expert in a wide range of related technologies. According to Henneberger, the need for IP protection is wider than one might ordinarily think.

"'Inventions' are not always a game changer, or a flash of genius," Henneberger says. "Most are improvements on existing technology, which need protection. It's usually a steady flow of such improvements that make up a patent portfolio, which is an extremely valuable resource that enhances valuation and can be used offensively or defensively— that is, to expand market share and drive competitors out, or to license the innovation and realize an enhanced revenue stream." Think of the patent, he says, like a deed to a piece of property, albeit one that reads like an engineering document that enhances valuation and boosts company morale.

Adds Winer, who earned a degree in life science engineering, majoring in human and microbial genetics, is registered to practice before the USPTO and has worked in industries ranging from information technology (IT) to health care: "It becomes increasingly important in highly competitive industries, such as electronics or health care. Here, the patent world is crowded, and carving out your cover is critical in a variety of ways. Investors, for example, want to keep competitors out. The claims have to be rock solid because, as the stakes rise, you can expect that the claims will come under attack," Winer adds.

Are there typical ways that otherwise savvy companies err, in terms of their everyday procedures? Winer notes that some companies "fail to document the invention properly. You want witnessed laboratory reports, photos of the invention, to help support the patent," he says, adding that a simple way to proceed with documentation is to make copies of the material and email or send the materials to yourself.

What is a patent, anyway? According to the experts at Hoffmann & Baron, LLP, a patent is a legal document granted by the federal government—the USPTO, to be exact—to the patent owner, granting the right to exclude others from making, using, selling, offering to sell, and importing the claimed invention. It's a property right to the inventor. Depending on the industry—and thus the backlog of applications—a patent is issued anywhere from about two to four years after the application is filed. "There is a rather large slush pile in some areas of technology," Henneberger says. A utility patent lasts for 20 years from the filing date.

What can be patented? Virtually anything made by mankind, from machines to human cells, from computer chips to DNA molecules. Patentable items also include methods of creating things. Let's get specific. According to the experts at Fleit Gibbons Gutman Bongini & Bianco PL, the statute provides that whoever invents or discovers any new and useful process, machine, manufacture, or composition of matter, or any new and useful improvement, may obtain a patent, subject to the terms and requirements of the patent statute. A "machine" is considered an apparatus such as an auto, television set, a computer or computer software, or a business method carried out by a machine. A "manufacture" is an article or object that is made by manufacturing, such as a light bulb, baseball bat, tire, or DVD.

Examples of a "composition of matter" include a chemical compound, candy bar, or sports drink. A "method" is a process such as a series of steps for making soap. There is often an overlap among these areas, but all that is required is that an invention qualifies under any of the preceding categories of invention.

What do the requirements that the invention be "new and useful" mean? First, under U.S. law, the invention must not only be new, it must also not be obvious. All that is required for an invention to be "new" is that it is different from what is already known. An invention is not "obvious" if a person of ordinary skill in the field of the invention would not have known how to make or use the invention without undue experimentation. In other words, our law does not permit the issuance of patents for trivial or routine modifications of known inventions.

Generally, an invention is "useful" if it works. There is no requirement that an invention be better than prior inventions. All that is required is that the invention performs some task. This is not generally difficult to establish.

I pause here for a brief Patent Office joke interlude:

> If you throw a patented object on grass, and the grass dies, the object is a defoliant. If the grass grows, it's fertilizer.

What is *not* patentable? Laws of nature. Physical phenomena. Abstract ideas. A suggestion. So, practically speaking, an idea or suggestion of a new machine is not patentable. A complete description of the actual machine or other subject matter for which the patent is sought is required.

Further, an invention cannot be patented if "(a) the invention was known or used by others in this country, or patented or described in a printed publication in this or a foreign country, before the invention thereof by the applicant for patent'' or ''(b) the invention was patented or described in a printed publication . . . (or) in public use or on sale in this country more than one year prior to the application for patent in the United States. . . . ''

Even if the subject matter sought to be patented is not exactly shown by the prior art, Henneberger explains, and involves one or more differences over the most nearly similar thing already known, a patent may still be refused if the differences would be obvious. The subject matter must be sufficiently different from what has been used or described before that it may be said to be nonobvious to a person having ordinary skill in the area of technology related to the invention.

For example, he says, making two component parts into a single component, or using different components that accomplish the same function (e.g., Velcro instead of snaps), is ordinarily not patentable.

There are two types of patents, Hoffmann & Baron's Henneberger explains:

- The first is a *utility patent*, which addresses functionality, that is, the way an article is used and works (35 U.S.C. 101).
- A *design patent* protects the way an article looks (35 U.S.C. 171), or ornamental appearance, such as shape and decoration.

According to Hoffmann & Baron, both design and utility patents may be obtained on an article if invention resides both in its utility and ornamental appearance. While utility and design patents afford legally separate protection, the utility and ornamentality of an article are not easily separable. Articles of manufacture, they note, may possess both functional and ornamental characteristics.

For the budding inventor, engineer, or entrepreneur, a cost-efficient way to begin the process is to do an online search first, via one of the web sites like www.google.com/patents. "For those with a big idea and limited experience and financial resources, do the search yourself to eliminate dead ends," says Winer. "When you see that an invention is 'close' but not exactly like yours, then you can bring in the IP attorney for the initial consultation."

Lots of technology has been patented that hasn't made it to the marketplace, advises Henneberger, and this initial "online research" step is a quick and inexpensive way to find out what is "out there." The patent system, he adds, can be effectively used by the canny entrepreneur. "There is a wealth of information in online patent databases, widget design A to Z," he notes. "You can also investigate a competitor's patent portfolio, which can help guide you in your product designs, such as identifying features of interest—and those to avoid, to steer clear of infringement conflicts."

What about placing related ideas under one patent application versus separate patents for each nuanced concept? This can be a balancing act. Winer notes: "The USPTO likes applications that are crystal clear. They like quick, easier-to-resolve applications, and, in terms of strategy, it can be better to do a nice, contained case, as opposed to an omnibus approach. But," he adds, "this is a strategy best mapped between you and your IP attorney."

Again, the application is a detailed description that includes claims that delineate the "subject matter" of the invention and defines it in a way so that it is distinguishable from previously existing products or methods. The claims section is critical to the success of the patent application—it defines the boundaries of the protection granted in the patent, according to Hoffmann & Baron's experts.

In the 1998 decision *In Re Hiniker,* the Court of Appeals for the Federal Circuit said: "The name of the game is the claim." Patent litigation can be won or lost on the basis of how patent claims are interpreted, according to Hoffmann & Baron's experts.

In fact, they note one particularly important case critical to the interpretation of patent claims language, the 2005 *Phillips v. AWH Corporation.* According to Hoffmann & Baron, the *en banc* decision of the Federal Circuit in *Phillips* (as reported in the September 2005 issue of *Managing Intellectual Property*) delineates general guidelines for interpretation in future cases. These guidelines include:

- *No rigid algorithm for interpreting claims.* The methodology to be used is determined by how best to achieve "a full understanding of what the inventors actually invented and intended to envelope with the claim."
- *Intrinsic evidence.* The specification is the primary source for construing the meaning of the claims; claim language, limitations in dependent claims, explicit definitions of claim terms and clear disavowals of scope in the specification, and, to a lesser extent, the prosecution history are paramount to claim interpretation.
- *Extrinsic evidence.* Dictionaries, treatises, and expert/inventor testimony may be useful in some circumstances, but are given less weight than intrinsic evidence.

- *Limitation of claim term.* A limitation of claim term should not be imported from the specification into the claims unless there is either an explicit, special definition given to the term by the patentee that differs from the meaning it would otherwise possess, or the specification reveals an explicit and clear intentional disclaimer of claim scope by the inventor.

Therefore, in drafting patent applications after *Phillips:*

- Carefully draft the specification and claims. Define the scope of each term used in the claims with great care in the specification. It is very important to make absolutely clear whether a claim term is intended to be given its ordinary meaning and, if not, precisely how it is to be understood.
- Ensure that the specification fully supports the broadest possible meaning of the claim terms.
- Provide more than one embodiment or species to support a claimed genus. Two embodiments or species are more than twice as good as one. The more, the better.
- Draft many dependent claims to confirm a generic interpretation of terms in an independent claim under the doctrine of claim differentiation.
- Make sure any objectives or advantages of the invention mentioned in the specification cannot be interpreted as limitations to the claimed invention.

(*Note:* I am not an attorney, nor do I play one on TV. As new case law comes into play, it becomes increasingly clear to me and my fellow innovators that a strong relationship with skillful IP attorney is an absolute must.)

Is it ever in the innovator's best interest *not* to apply for patent protection? The patent makes your invention public, and you may decide, in consultation with your IP attorney, that the best strategy is to maintain your invention as a *trade secret*.

With manufacturing and/or assembly technologies, for example, patenting exposes details to your competitors, and it can be difficult to check or verify usage.

Laws governing trade secrets vary from state to state, but in most states, two basic requirements must be met: (1) demonstration that there is economic value from not having the invention publicly known, and (2) "reasonable" efforts must be made to maintain the secrecy of the information.

Is there a disadvantage to this approach? According to Hoffmann & Baron, the trade secret owner theoretically can keep the information "secret" indefinitely. However, wily competitors can discover this trade secret via reverse engineering. And in hot industries, or when the stakes are high, you can expect the wolves out there to try to huff and puff and blow your house down. And these wolves have increasingly advanced analytical tools at their disposal. It is getting harder and harder to keep trade secrets "secret."

## Frequently Asked Questions

Discussions with attorneys Henneberger and Winer unearth questions they regularly field from budding inventors and long-time innovators alike. Now that I have addressed the basics of IP, let's examine some of these most-asked questions on IP, patents, and process.

### What is meant by "patent pending" and "patent applied for"?

According to the USPTO, these are terms used by a manufacturer or seller of an article to inform the public that an application for patent on that article is on file. The law imposes a fine on those who use these terms falsely to deceive the public, so a word to the wise.

### What's the chance that the USPTO will give others info from my application while it's pending?

Again, according to the USPTO, most patent applications will be published 18 months after the filing date of the application. If a nonpublication request is filed in a timely manner, patent applications are "maintained in the strictest confidence until the patent is issued or the application is published." After publication, copies of the application file may be requested by the public. After the patent is issued, the office file containing the application and all correspondence relevant to the issuance of the patent is made available for public review; copies of these files may be obtained from the Patent Office.

### If two (or more) persons collaborate on an invention, to whom will the patent be granted?

If each had a share in the ideas forming the invention as defined in the claims—even if only as to one claim—they are joint inventors and a patent will be issued to them jointly on the basis of a proper patent application, according to the USPTO. However, if one of these persons provided all of the ideas of the invention, and the other followed instructions in making it, the person who contributed ideas is the sole inventor, and the patent application will be in his/her name only.

### What is a trademark ($^{TM}$) or servicemark($^{SM}$)?

According to Hoffmann & Baron's team of experts, a trademark is a word, name, symbol, or device that is used in trade with goods to indicate the source of origin of the goods and to distinguish them from the goods of others. A service mark is the same as a trademark, with the exception that it identifies and distinguishes the source of origin of a service rather than a product. The terms *trademark* and *mark* are commonly used to refer to both trademarks and service marks.

As to trademark rights, these may be used to prevent others from using a confusingly similar mark, but not to prevent others from making the same goods, or from selling the same goods or services under a clearly different mark. Trademarks that are used in interstate or foreign commerce may be registered with the USPTO.

The registration procedure for trademarks and general information concerning trademarks is described online at the USPTO web site (see "Basic Facts about Trademarks," www.uspto.gov/web/offices/tac/doc/basic/).

### What is a copyright (©)?

A copyright is a form of protection provided to the authors of "original works of authorship," including literary, dramatic, musical, artistic, and certain other intellectual works, both published and un-published. The owner of the copyright has the exclusive right to reproduce the work, prepare derivative works, distribute copies or recordings of the work, perform the work publicly, or display the copyrighted work publicly, according to the 1976 Copyright Act.

A copyright protects the form of expression, rather than the subject matter of the writing, Hoff-mann & Baron explains. For example, a written description of a machine can be copyrighted, but this would only prevent others from copying the description; it would not prevent others from writing a description of their own, or from making and using the machine. Copyrights are registered by the Copyright Office of the Library of Congress. Want to file yourself? Ask your attorney's advice, but be sure to visit www.copyright.gov as well.

Now we get into some nitty-gritty areas that have vexed innovation-driven executives around the country. Special thanks to patent attorney Gary Winer and the IP minds at Fleit Gibbons Gutman Bongini & Bianco PL for the following information.

### Can I lose my rights to patent after inventing?

Yes. First if you publish the invention in writing or make a product embodying the invention and sell it or use it publicly more than one year before filing a patent application covering the invention. In that case, you have lost your right to patent in the United States.

In addition, many countries have laws that provide that an inventor who publishes the invention before filing an application covering that invention has lost his/her right to patent. And there are other instances and situations that may also lead to loss of rights to patent. Consult your IP professional.

**Why should I patent my inventions?**

The chief reason: to make money from the invention. In the ultimate analysis, obtaining a patent is not worth the time, effort, and money if nobody else will ever use the patented invention. However, if an invention is successful, it will be imitated, and if the invention is not patented, the inventor will not participate in the profits of his or her competitors. Investors in companies recognize this and will seldom invest in companies that do not protect their inventions and aggressively patrol their patents.

**What can I do against infringers before my patent issues?**

In order to sue, one must have an issued patent. However, negotiations on a license can begin before issuance. Word to the wise: Keep it secret and avoid public disclosure until the patent issues.

**Can I begin marketing my invention before I get the patent?**

Yes, but be sure to disclose ideas under a confidentiality agreement. Even then, there is no substitute for filing a patent application. A confidentiality agreement is no guarantee that this critical information will not be made public. If a person receiving information subject to a confidentiality agreement makes the information public, some rights may be lost by the inventor. Worse, all the inventor may have left is a lawsuit against the person breaching the confidentiality agreement.

**Do I absolutely need an attorney or patent agent to apply for a patent?**

Get the professional help you need to prepare the patent application. This is not a fill-in form. Drafting a powerful patent application requires creativity and savvy, and the ability to negotiate with the USPTO on the scope of the claims, among other things.

Remember, "the name of the game is the claim." The key task of the patent attorney is determining the scope of the invention and expressing that scope by drafting claims that define the invention. The inventor, experience shows, is usually not the best judge of the scope of the invention.

Remember, too, that getting a patent issued is easier than successfully asserting the patent against an infringer. Infringers seldom agree that they infringe and commonly resist the patent owners' efforts to license the patent. The higher the stakes, the greater the intensity of the attacks (this bears repeating). Therefore, the patent application must be a carefully created legal document designed to pass muster with the USPTO that is constructed in an ironclad fashion to withstand withering assaults from infringers (and their lawyers).

Another point on this matter: the USPTO routinely rejects claims for being too broad. Yet, unnecessarily narrow claims will allow others to use the invention, without infringing the claims. Seeking the services of a good patent attorney is generally the best course to take.

### Is software patentable?

Yes, inventions embodied in computer programs can be protected with patents. Patents protect the physical embodiments of inventions. Computer programs, like any other useful article, may or may not embody inventions. It is important to understand that patents protect inventions, and these inventions may be embodied in many different products. A computer program loaded into a general-purpose computer converts the computer into a specialized apparatus. Additionally, the same invention may be implemented in an apparatus that is specifically made to carry out the invention. A good patent would cover both of these embodiments, and perhaps others as well.

### Can I reserve a trademark?

In the United States, one acquires rights to a trademark by using the mark. There is no procedure for reserving a mark. However, a person who has a bona fide intention to use a trademark, under circumstances showing the good faith of such person, may apply to register the mark on the principal register of the USPTO. This is called an intent-to-use application, and even in this case, an applicant for registration of the mark must show use of the trademark within six months after the date, when a notice of allowance of the registration is issued.

Such a showing requires a specimen or facsimile of the mark as used in commerce, and a verified statement that the mark is in use in commerce and specifying the date of the applicant's first use of the mark in commerce. In these cases, an applicant should make sure that the mark is the same as the one set forth in the application for registration.

### Do I need to register my trademark?

Using a trademark first, in a given territory, establishes some rights in its user. However, there are important advantages to registration of the trademark in the principal register of the USPTO. It is also possible to register a trademark in some states. A certificate of registration in the PTO has the effect of being prima facie evidence of validity of the registered mark.

### Should I register in other countries?

More businesses today have an international component to their sales than ever before, accelerated in part by Internet usage. Careful consideration should be given to selection and protection of the appropriate marks in various countries.

### Should I do an availability search on the mark prior to using it?

The firm recommends to its clients that they have an availability search performed before using a mark, for a variety of reasons. First, if a search is not performed and you start using a mark, that use may infringe the mark of another person. Further, a court could find the infringement to be willful, resulting in higher penalties.

## Do patents and trademarks protect against counterfeiters?

Here, we access the expertise of Rick Van Arnam, partner at Barnes, Richardson & Colburn, global trade law practitioners. According to Van Arnam, many companies are not aware of the steps they need to take to protect their valuable IP against counterfeiting and other unauthorized use.

It sometimes seems as if customs agents seize shipments of counterfeit goods every day, in ports from Long Beach, California, to Newark, New Jersey. And there are *many* links in the supply chain that are compromised, Van Arnam explains, from the importers of the bogus merchandise to freight forwarders, customs brokers, owners of warehouses, and so on.

What steps can patent and trademark holders take to safeguard this valuable IP? According to Van Arnam and the practitioners at Barnes, Richardson & Colburn, there are six key points to be aware of:

1. Register all your trademarks and patents in all the countries in which you do business, plan to do business, or could conceivably do business— either selling or sourcing. Trademark laws are territorial, so merely filing in the United States or the European Union will not safeguard you in other countries. You can help prevent trademark pirates from beating you to the trademark

office in a country you now decide to do business in by using foresight as to which markets you could potentially enter and registering your marks in those countries.

2. Register your trademarks and trade names with U.S. Customs and Border Protection (CBP). "I continue to see many companies fail to take this easy and inexpensive step that can lead to government interdiction at the border," Van Arnam says. If counterfeit merchandise is seized, CBP will advise you of the names and addresses of the exporter and importer, allowing you the possibility of taking additional steps directly against the offending party.

3. Know your vendors and manufacturers. They are making your product, and you need to be sure that they are not making additional units of your merchandise on the side.

4. Be aggressive with the law. Many remedies exist, in both civil and criminal law, and at both the federal and state court levels. No violation is too small to warrant, at a minimum, a cease-and-desist letter.

5. Identify web sites, especially auction sites, selling counterfeit merchandise. Become familiar with the auction house policies allowing legitimate rights holders to identify themselves and to have the auction house remove offending auctions. For example, on eBay this is called Verified Rights Owner Program; on Sell.com it is called the Rights Owner Compliance Systems.

6. Educate your employees on these issues so that they understand the importance of protecting your company's valuable IP rights.

## Remember: The Wolves Are Always at the Door

In summary, I strongly suggest a robust approach to all issues related to IP. Identifying and working with highly qualified legal experts takes time and money. Experience tells me that it is time and money very well spent. I urge you to vigorously protect your firm's IP and use IP professionals to safeguard your innovations. Marketing, prudent business measures, and IP—properly cared for and fed—will help you grow your business and box out the many competitors who are all too ready to attack.

### Think About

- Who handles your organization's patent applications and the "care and feeding" of your IP portfolio?
- When was your last patent? What was it for?
- Have you experienced any recent patent infringement–related issues? What was the outcome?
- Have you experienced any recent product counterfeiting issues? What was the outcome?

# CHAPTER 7

# Innovation Implementation

Innovation is the ability to successfully convert ideas into value-added outcomes for your company, customers, shareholders, and others. Or, as innovation expert Nic Hunt puts it: "Successful innovation is turning ideas into money."

Expressed as a mathematical formula, implementing innovation is:

| Ability to define innovation in a manner that makes strategic sense for *your* organization | + | Know-how to properly construct and use a process | + | Will to keep the process on course |
|---|---|---|---|---|

= That's sustainable innovation.

## Getting Started

There's more to the new product development (NPD) process than creating a sleek brainstorming room with wildly painted walls, a foosball table, beanbag chairs,

133

crayons, construction paper, and Etch-A-Sketches strewn about. Even in a well-intentioned venue like this, a creative person can hit a dead end, waiting for that *"Eureka!"* moment, the would-be Archimedes lying on the industrially carpeted brainstorming room floor, staring at the soundproof tiles, stumped.

Innovation implementation is built upon a robust, disciplined strategy that helps identify and deliver these "value-added outcomes." And not just one time—lightning in a bottle—but over and over again, so that a new wave of innovation is always behind the one preceding, ready to crest even as the earlier innovation matures. Thus, the steady flow of innovation, over time, sustains above-average, long-term profitability.

Building this strategy means that you, at the steering wheel of this process, must:

- Define the type of innovation you really need most in your organization—what it is you hope to achieve.
- Manage expectations and set the stage for both failure and success.
- Complete the audit process.
- Assemble the right team—smart, diverse, and committed—and understand the keys to motivating this unique group.
- Get C-level buy-in and active participation.
- Strive for a few quick, early "wins" as work continues on "game-breaking" innovations.

Says Jeff Ackerberg, president and CEO, Grohe America, "Any company can have one or two innovations, over a period of time. However, to be true innovators, it's essential to have an appropriately robust, structured innovation strategy. A market-driven strategic vision must be in place, and there needs to be consensus over how the brand is going to differentiate itself in the marketplace. This brings focus, with a road map, screening criteria, and checkpoints. If a project doesn't fulfill the brand strategy, it should be dropped."

I agree. Implementing innovation is about taking the organization and doing a "reboot." It has to be done methodically, with care, and it takes time. More time than filling a room with balloons, Legos, and strange furniture, calling it the innovation center, and inviting team members in to "create."

Mention *structure* to some folks and they quake. Some believe that *structure* and *creativity* are mutually exclusive. I disagree. My opinion is that the organizations that successfully innovate, over time, chart a course between discipline and pure, untethered creativity, using powerful processes and ever mindful of applying Robert's Rules of Innovation. Experience tells me that rather than dampen the creative spirit, structure actually frees it. Remember, too, that "structure" runs along a sliding scale, from "simple" to "sophisticated," depending on the needs and wants of the organization.

"Innovation implementation is not a one-size-fits-all proposition," says Jeff DeFazio. "The process and the role of the team itself evolves with the needs, size, and culture of the organization."

Before we proceed, let's ask ourselves: Categorically, what is *not* considered innovation? If you're a product manufacturer, you might consider such items as:

- Changes to materials that offer nearly identical products, for the purpose of offering dual sourcing.

- Changes to the process that require technical validation for an identical (or nearly identical) product
  (such as validating a replacement tool).
- A change that a customer can alter, from run to run,
  for a change fee (such as a print design).
- Existing products produced for a particular market
  that can be sold, unaltered, in another market category that would fall under the heading of "business
  development opportunity."

## Define Your Organization's Needs

The key to successful innovation implementation is,
appropriately enough, defining the types of innovation
and looking at organization needs. Sometimes, innovation
is hard to define because it is used so often to refer to
many types of innovation, from minor product or service
improvements to the transformative or breakthrough
innovation.

The hardest kind of innovation to manage—and the
one with the greatest potential—is transformative, which
creates an entirely new way to deliver value. Yet it is often
pursued in the same manner as the incremental
innovation.

Most so-called innovations are incremental, which can
mean a new way of doing business, a new process, an
exciting new brand feature—even an alliance with a trade
partner.

Innovation turns ideas into money, as Nic Hunt says. If
the "invention" is a process that reduces costs, helps
expand our business, and enhances productivity, well, that's
a good thing. In fact, experience shows that many companies are actually focusing on innovations that positively

impact the bottom line, doing the same thing, only cheaper, easier, or faster. They can actually fund development of new products to accelerate top-line growth and can be easier and faster to achieve than the earth-shattering breakthrough, thus building early support.

And yet vigorous pursuit of "home run" innovations is critical to long-term viability. A 2003 London School of Business innovation study shows that organizations that focus solely on incremental product or service enhancement cannot stem decline in their own market as they mature and new players enter the field. In fact, most organizations do not focus resources on building an innovation pipeline for entirely new forms of products and services.* Most concentrate:

- 80 percent of their resources on incremental improvements to existing markets.
- 10 percent on incremental improvements to new markets.
- 10 percent on radical innovation to new markets.

Let's examine the various types of innovation, shown in Exhibit 7.1, with examples of each:

- *Transformative (disruptive)* Few and far between, these are game changers, which leave competitors scrambling. Typically, they open entirely new businesses or markets. Think about these, as examples:
  - ◆ Product: a flying car
  - ◆ Service: Internet banking

---

*See www.freethinkr.wordpress.com for more information.

**Exhibit 7.1    Levels and Types of Innovation**

| Level of Innovation | Product | Service | Process | Business Model |
|---|---|---|---|---|
| **Breakthrough** (Disruptive) | Flying car | Internet banking | Assembly line | Internet |
| **Differential** (Expanding) | Alternative energy (hydrogen) | New kind of mortgage | Custom build tracking (RIDF) | Onlines sales and distribution |
| **Incremental** (Sustaining) | New car model | Different mortgage feature | Online tracking | Factory outlets |

*Source:* www.innovationcoach.com.

- ◆ Process: assembly line
- ◆ Business model: Internet
- *Radical (architectural).* When a radical innovation appears, competitors want to copy it immediately. These are practices new to the industry, which overturn long-established ways of operating. Examples:
  - ◆ Product: hydrogen-powered cars
  - ◆ Service: new mortgage product
  - ◆ Process: custom build tracking (RIDF)
  - ◆ Business model: online sales and distribution
- *Incremental.* This most commonplace type of innovation is typically a tweak to an existing product, process, or service. The incremental innovation raises the bar slightly or becomes the industry standard. For example:
  - ◆ Product: a new car model
  - ◆ Service: a different mortgage feature
  - ◆ Process: online tracking
  - ◆ Business model: factory outlets

## Open Innovation: Light Bulb

A quick example of a neat innovation? The venerable incandescent light bulb. This is an industry near and dear to me, given my experience early on with Philips and, later, with Sylvania Lighting. In 2007, Congress passed tough new efficiency standards for 2012—so tough that many thought the death knell for "regular" incandescent light bulbs was finally sounding.

This sparked an innovation race within the industry to create a better incandescent. Lo and behold, Philips has already launched a bulb that retails for around $5 each (versus as little as 25 cents for standard-issue bulbs). Touted as 30 percent more efficient and lasting three times as long, the new bulbs have the light quality consumers favor, versus some very efficient compact fluorescent bulbs. The new bulbs are already a retail hit, reports the *New York Times* (July 6, 2009), and "a wave of innovation appears to be coming," the story states.

Then, says Nic Hunt, there needs to be a clear business strategy. "Within this," he says, "the contribution of innovation to the delivery of the strategy must be quantified. The innovation pipeline should be developed to match this goal."

It is important, in other words, to define innovation, in the context of the organization. What do you hope to achieve with your innovation program? What are the expectations? Do you intend to focus on both "internal" and "external" innovations? Once developed, the strategy can be fed to the team, digested, and absorbed—the group is on the same page, with a shared vision. It is an essential part of building the innovation culture.

This up-front work—defining innovation—is critical. It's the difference between setting a course and reacting once you realize you're off-course. Proactive, rather than reactive. This proactivity, this focus, frees your team to concentrate on execution—they know where the goal line is.

Remember, too, that CEO, board, and/or leadership support is vital to the success of the innovation program. I have to say, and I think my worldwide network of innovators would agree, if the big dogs don't buy into it, don't do it.

Make sure your audit process is complete. You need to understand where your organization is at, now, as well as have a sense of where you need to go, how far you need to climb. If you are unsure of your innovation status, review the short audit, online, at www.innovationcoach.com/solutions/ short-audit. It provides a visual impression of the areas that may need attention and improvement. For a comprehensive, 10-dimensional rating that corresponds with Robert's Rules of Innovation, go to www.innovation coach.com/ solutions/online-in-depth-audit/. (See Exhibit 7.2.)

Manage expectations and set the stage for flops because, as I've said, there will and should be failures. Having said that, make sure your successes are properly "merchandised" (i.e., communicated) to both internal and external audiences. In terms of best practices, a great tip is to knock off some quick, relatively easy wins to build equity for your innovation program. To use a baseball analogy, make sure you play "small ball"—moving the runners station to station to manufacture runs—well. A couple of quick runs will get attention for the program, build morale company-wide, and result in early traction for the program from those up on high in your organization.

## NPD Process in Action

The NPD process, while critical to the success of the innovation program, is often misunderstood and can

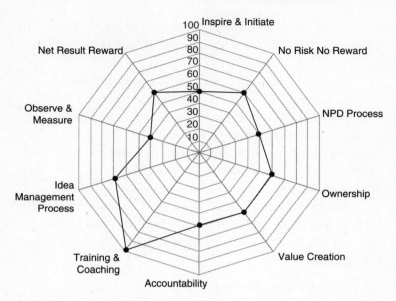

**Exhibit 7.2    In-Depth Online Audit Example**

*Source:* www.innovationcoach.com/chart-long/chart.php.

seem daunting to the uninitiated. Many savvy and highly successful business leaders eschew complex processes. Entrepreneurial by nature, such women and men achieve repeat successes thanks to their unerring understanding of their marketplace and remarkable instincts.

We spoke recently with Walter Hester, the hugely successful owner and founder of Maui Jim, the sunglasses manufacturer renowned for its cool "Aloha" styling, quality optics, and PolarizedPlus2$^{TM}$ lens technology. Maui Jim is the fastest-growing and the largest privately owned maker of polarized sunglasses in the world.

"Walter," we asked, "what's your NPD process like?"

"I'm it," he said.

Walter and his team know the market, know the customers, and know what the retailers like. It's in their DNA.

"I put myself in the customer's shoes and ask: 'Is that feature something I would pay $5 or $10 more for?'"

Not everyone is as savvy and successful, however. Lesser mortals need the structure of a detailed, formalized NPD process. Some of these are branded, well-known formats. Others are hybrids forged by successful executives to meet the needs of their organizations the world over.

Exhibit 7.3 offers one example, from our friend Jeff DeFazio. It makes a lot of good sense and has served Jeff well over the years. The process is basically divided into three stages:

1. Production Definition
2. Qualification
3. Revenue

In the product definition stage (1), a wide funnel is built to pull concepts from key constituents, including sales, vendors, and marketing. These concepts undergo a rigorous marketing department review. Does it fit with brand strategy? The company's image? What's the profit potential? How does it fare given the competitive environment? If the concept passes muster, marketing collaborates with sourcing to identify and adapt products—or create new ones.

Still a go? If so, the concept becomes a "new item proposal" (NIP); the market opportunity it represents is quantified, in terms of potential sales and return relative to investment. At this point, the NIP is reviewed: It may go back a step for refinement, or relegated to the NIP

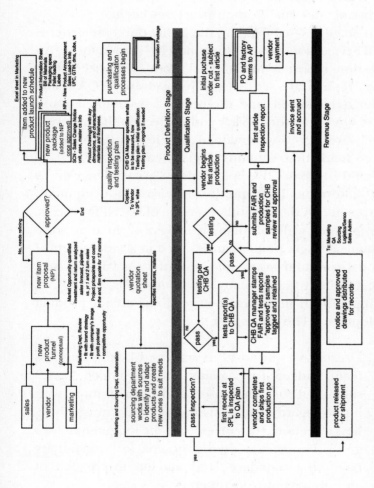

**Exhibit 7.3  Product Development Process Flow, Example I**

*Source:* Jeff DeFazio.

graveyard if it's a clear "no." Or, if approved, it moves on to become a new product package (NPP). It is added to the new product launch schedule. It is quality tested. The purchasing and qualification processes begin.

In Stage 2, Qualification, the initial purchase order is cut. The vendor begins "first article" production. An inspection report is made. The product is tested. If it passes, reports are sent to quality assurance (QA). The vendor is contacted, and the product is completed and sent to QA for further review and inspection. If approved, samples are tagged and retained, with information distributed to marketing, sourcing, logistics, and sales.

Failure to pass? Bye-bye vendor. Passed? Then on to Stage 3, Revenue. Here, product is released for shipment.

Appendix A shows another version of the NPD process, the one I used while at Airspray, makers of the innovative mechanical finger-pump foamers used in a wide variety of personal care and household products. As you can see, there are many stages, many test points.

Appendix B shows a five-stage flowchart for product development. The stages are:

1. *Dream.* A "wild idea" is screened by the business team, judged for viability and, if judged "yes," submitted for comparison and prioritization, with inputs regarding market analytics and strategic business direction. (It is dropped if the judgment is "no go.") The dream then proceeds for preliminary research (secondary data) and on to creation of an "opportunity document."

2. *Discover.* Next is the project kickoff meeting and concept model. A preliminary project plan is created, market research and a competitive analysis

undertaken, and preliminary costing estimated before heading to a viability analysis (go/no go). If yes, the business development plan is created, along with a project plan. Then, another approval stage. If it's still a go, we head to . . .

3. *Design.* Concepts are refined, as necessary, and a design criteria document prepared (and validation research undertaken). A final design is submitted for approval by the product manager. (*IP Alert:* At this point, file your patents!) Once approved, it joins the preliminary tooling estimates (which are submitted for a Level B product costing review) and market validation for a project review by the business team, at which point we hit another go/no-go milestone. And, if it's still a go . . .

4. *Develop.* A variety of plans are created (commercialization, quality, tooling, packaging, components, manufacturing and distribution, costing), along with computer-aided design (CAD) modeling, prototyping, and product documentation—and synthesized into another review package, where the next go/no-go milestone occurs. Here, we either loop back for refinements or proceed to Stage 5 . . .

5. *Deliver.* Where tools and fixtures are ordered, first shot samples are created, to pilot production, mold release, inventory, LAUNCH!—followed by an audit of results.

Appendix C shows a six-step system, which we adapted at a major multinational, multi-product-line company. The first graphic depicts the intent and scope of activities in each stage, while the second shows the "key enablers" for each stage. In the third, we show the relative volume of

**Exhibit 7.4    Simple NPD Process**

| Stage | Ideation | Development | Scale Up | Launch |
| --- | --- | --- | --- | --- |
| Concept 1 | | | | |
| Concept 2 | | | | |
| Concept 3 | | | | |

involvement of one of five company interest groups: sales, marketing, legal, technical, and financial.

Overwhelmed? Exhibit 7.4 boils it down to a four-step "Simple NPD Process" that will take you from ideation to launch! The basic idea, however, is to combine, as Nic Hunt explains, a "boundless ideation process with a targeted effort aligned to the business strategy."

The idea "hopper" is most effective, he says, when actively managed. "Segmentation, valuation, and selection processes ensure that the most appropriate ideas that deliver what the business strategy requires are selected.

## Creating a Road Map to Success

From these examples, what becomes clear is how a structured, transparent process can efficiently manage groups of products and keep projects flowing. The key elements are:

- *Quality.* Hunt refers to the optimal selection of projects that, if successful, will deliver the best strategic outcome for the invested funds.
- *Capability.* This refers to how individual projects are managed and tracked through the system.

- *Capacity*. How well the organization can manage and prioritize resources to support a portfolio of well-managed (or "capable") projects.

And, again, the degree of complexity of the NPD process, and the scope of the innovation team's role, stretches across an infinite range and depends on the organization.

Where this is all relatively new, and the culture is still evolving, the innovation team may be the company's innovation hatchery. They help clarify situations, define problems and identify opportunities, and facilitate the process. In a sense, the innovation team is an internal agency, servicing internal clients, in various groups.

No matter what NPD process format is used, it is imperative that the stages are clearly defined, as are the tasks within each stage. This is, after all, your road map for success.

## Guidelines for Progress

Today's savvy organizations that have standardized their process are, over time, modifying their approach to NPD development processes in several important ways. In terms of best practices regarding innovation implementation, as it relates to the NPD process itself, I've collected these insights and tips from colleagues around the world and present them to you here:

- *Do we go/no go?* Today, the decision makers of go/no go are clearly defined and teams are streamlined, with more systematic approaches to effective decision making. This stage is given sharper teeth than ever before. Stick to the agreed-upon go/no-go criteria. Leave "gut feelings" for the weekly football pool. Importantly, though, the no-go projects are dropped into an idea bank for modification and/or tinkering at a later date. Dr. Robert G. Cooper is a thought leader in the field of innovation management and creator of the Stage-Gate new product process (www .stage-gate.com). Says Dr. Cooper: "Perhaps the greatest challenge that users of a stage and gate process face is making the gates work. As go the gates, so goes the process." In a robust gating system, poor projects are spotted early and killed. Projects in trouble are detected and sent back for rework.

- *No free passes.* Another word on go/no go—no freebies for top-level execs who might try to ramrod through a pet project. All projects get the same scrutiny—no exceptions! Everyone plays by the same rules. Got it, Mr. CEO?

- *Ah, bucket.* Improvements have been made in creating "strategic buckets" to achieve the right balance and mix of projects, scorecards to make better go/no-go decisions, and usage of the productivity index (a financial approach based upon the theory of constraints) to help prioritize projects and allocate resources.

- *Lean, mean, and scalable.* Dr. Cooper notes the value of keeping the system nimble, through new methods such as value stream analysis (from lean manufacturing), spiral (or agile) development through a series of "build, test, feedback, and revise" iterations, flexible discretion over which activities are executed, simultaneous executions of key activities and even stages, multiple versions scaled to suit different types and risk levels of projects, and multiple versions for platform/technology development projects.

- *The rearview mirror review.* For many successful innovators, here's the secret (shhhh)—*it's all about key learnings.* Organizations are doing launch post-mortems, with performance metrics in place, to measure project performance, establish team accountability, and build in improvements for the future. "Next generation Stage-Gate systems build in a rigorous postlaunch review, in order to instill accountability for results and foster a culture of continuous improvement," he says.

- *Feed the funnel.* Organizations are incorporating a "discovery phase" to help feed the innovation funnel. Today, there is more opportunity for experimentation and toggling back and forth, as well as less reliance on financial go/no-go criteria and more on strategic criteria. In uncertain times, certainly the temptation is to kill off projects based primarily on money issues. However, this approach truly is anathema to those seeking longer-term, or sustainable, innovation.

## Think About

- What is your organization's innovation strategy?
- Are your innovations typically transformative? Radical? Incremental?
- On which category is most of your team's efforts spent?
- How sharp are the teeth on your NPD process gates?
- Does your CEO get a free pass on his or her pet projects?

# 8

# Innovation Checklist

The playing field has changed, and competitors around the world are nipping at your heels. And, as I've said, too many organizations figure the way to fight back is to cut prices, by cutting costs. Addition by subtraction—and one of the items to go is innovation.

Innovate or die.

If you've read this far, you understand that sustainable innovation represents your organization's salvation, not an easily found line item to be excised from the budget.

In this final chapter, I briefly go through each of Robert's Rules of Innovation again, this time with an eye toward hard-core, practical tips and reminders designed to help you get on the road to sustainable innovation.

Then I offer "Advice from the Pros," a roundtable discussion featuring input from some of my associates, who offer commentary and advice for those ready to seriously dig into sustainable innovation.

Finally, some parting reminders before you head off to success through sustainable innovation.

## Preflight Preparation

An executive knows whether the organization's sustainable innovation effort is coming up short. You know you're in trouble if you're up in the middle of the night thinking about these strategy-related issues:

- "I'm not sure what products to focus on . . . "
- "What's our overarching vision regarding innovation?"
- "Our strategic plan is not 'strategic'—it's a static financial picture of our current situation."
- "Strategy implementation is unclear, right down to specific roles and functions . . . "

Or, if you are concerned about leadership issues, such as:

- "What is our culture of innovation, our vision?"
- "We're paying lip service to innovation—it's just words, not actionable . . . "
- "Decision-making processes are positively glacial— we can't deliver quickly . . . "
- "There's no cross-communication regarding innovation; we're in silos."

Or in terms of innovation team structure, competencies, and skills:

- "Risky ideas are avoided . . . "
- "There is way too much internal competition—the prevailing attitude: 'It's not my job.' "

- "Success isn't rewarded or internally communicated—or celebrated; we perform when we're forced to, because of specific marketplace situations."
- "Come to think of it, failure isn't communicated either . . ."
- "IP is not valued properly; a customer patented our idea."
- "There's a disconnect between both marketing and innovation and marketing and our customers."
- "We're great at manufacturing, but as inventors . . . ?"

If these are some of the things that prove worrisome to you regarding your organization's innovation programming, you can be assured of one thing:

You're not alone.

Here's how I see the plan for sustainable innovation. The **vision** leads to the **mission**, from which is developed the **strategy**. Inject vibrant **ideas** into the mix, and stir, with **climate and culture**, **process**, **technology**, and more, and voila—sustainable innovation. (See Exhibit 8.1.)

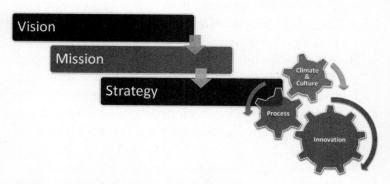

**Exhibit 8.1    Sustainable Innovation Model**

## Inspire

There are five key steps to achieve the type of innovation culture that inspires and creates intraorganization cohesion:

1. *Lead by example.* It all starts at the top. Management buy-in and support of innovation and ideation is critical. And by support, I mean both material and emotional. It needs not only to endorse but proactively push for innovation. It's the only way for your team to get the motivation to take time from their "day jobs" to make innovation happen.

2. *Overcommunicate, underpromise.* Talk up overarching innovation visions and successes (and failures), without hyperbole or pie-in-the-sky verbiage. Keep it simple. Keep it focused. Keep it real. Internal and external communications enhance group buy-in to innovation goals. It's important to articulate your grand vision and provide the compelling case for change.

3. *Two-way traffic:* Remember that communication of ideas is a two-way street. Open the door widely to encourage everyone to pipe up. *All* levels.

4. *Silo demolition:* Knock down the barriers that keep silos apart by creating cross-functional teams between groups that don't typically interact. This keeps the flame of cooperation—and innovation—burning brightly. "Silo-itis" can smother buy-in for innovation.

5. *Pick the right champions.* Select innovation champions from various groups, and provide ownership

and accountability, to drive innovation results. Raise the bar on your talent selections. You know who they are—recruit these superstars, now! And remember that even the most technical of innovations require leaders with superior people and communications skills.

**No Risk, No Innovation**

To increase initiative and innovation, you have to encourage—even embrace—failure. A culture that punishes less-than-stellar outcomes will stifle your program for sustainable innovation.

Here are five simple steps for encouraging initiative and innovation:

1. *Profiles in risk.* Clearly communicate the risk profile you are asking your people to adopt and state why it is important to the organization's success.
2. *Failure management.* Never allow an unsuccessful risk to hamper a team member's opportunities and advancement.
3. *Gold stars.* Create and communicate the results of an award program created with a high intraorganizational profile. It should, ideally, reward risks that pay off and "gee, nice try's" that don't.
4. *Key learnings process.* Establish a formalized, non-accusatory process for harvesting key learnings from unsuccessful risks. Distribute these lessons learned.
5. *Tools of the trade.* Give your people the situational risk assessment tools they need to help them improve their risk-taking decisions.

**New Product Development Process**[*]

Remember, "creative" and "structured" need not be mutually exclusive concepts:

- *Open wide.* Keep the idea funnels wide open. As Stage-Gate's Dr. Cooper advises, find and fill the product "white spaces"—untapped marketplace opportunities.
- *Sharpen those teeth.* Make sure your go/no-go decision checkpoints have "teeth."
- *It's not all about the money.* Think more in terms of strategic criteria versus financial for go/no-go decisions.
- *Nice try, Mr. Big Shot.* No "free passes" for C-level pet projects—all concepts undergo the same rigorous process.
- *Widen the innovation highway.* Make the system lean, adaptive, flexible, and scalable, in order so you can simultaneously process different types and risk levels of projects.
- *Share the knowledge.* Build in to the process a robust postlaunch review phase, to collect key learnings— and then make sure these are shared with the troops—invaluable for future successes.

---

[*]Robert G. Cooper, "How Companies Are Reinventing Their Idea-to-Launch Methodologies," *Research Technology Management*, March–April 2009, 52(2): 47–57.

##  Ownership

Everyone involved needs to feel truly part of the process and it's incumbent on the driver to knock down "us-versus-them" roadblocks in cross-divisional teams. To wit:

- *Who's driving this thing?* Your program for sustainable innovation must have a champion, a true driver of the process.
- *Where's the passion?* Select associates who care and are truly passionate about the product and the effort. Kick disbelievers off the bus—this is too important for naysayers to derail.
- *Different strokes for different folks.* Assign a specific task to a dedicated "owner"—this is critical to unleashing the best performance out of each member of the project team.
- *Follow up, feverishly.* Systematically and regularly follow up on action points from the previous team meeting. Review and assess status of the related deliverable.

**Value Creation**

In the discussion of optimizing sustainable innovation programs, here is the key: value creation. The real challenge, to me, is successfully managing the process and ensuring that the positive outcome results in superior return on investment (ROI).

Isn't ideation important? Of course. But, ultimately, the idea is to get a payback. A financial payback. Remember:

- *A means to an end.* Think of innovation as a process that uses intellectual capital to generate positive business results and, in the process, new findings— which spurs more innovation, and leads to further financial returns, and so on.
- *Key considerations.* As you track cash flow over time, remember to monitor start-up costs, speed to market, scale to volume, and other metrics.
- *The customer is king.* The value proposition is the key to successful innovation. Develop an innovation with high perceived value to your customer, and strong sales will follow.
- *IP protection.* Part of the three-legged stool (technology–business acumen–law) I referenced in Chapter 6 IP and patent protection locks in your competitive advantage that supports the sales results and market share increases that result in overall stakeholder value.

**Accountability**

A sustainable innovation program with accountability should be a goal of every innovation champion. Think of the benefits:

- *Stress reduction.* Accountability pushes your stress downward. You know you can count on your people. And your people know that the innovation champion is counting on them. Sleep—remember sleep? Accountability will help you get some.
- *Get out of the weeds.* When your team members are held accountable, time is freed for you, the team champion to concentrate on bigger picture, strategic elements. You're not down in the weeds anymore.
- *Full-tilt productivity.* Accountability means a team that is freed to work at full-performance levels. Confident, motivated, and engaged, they can focus on the business at hand, resulting in enhanced contributions.
- *Trust and respect.* Team members understand what is required of them, what is expected of them, which breeds intrateam trust and respect.
- *Accountability.* Its importance goes without saying but can be extremely tricky to inculcate. As you, the innovation champion, build a culture of innovation, consider these methods, which I've found extremely powerful.
- *Give them enough rope to.* . . . The natural tendency is to dictate terms—deadlines, methodologies, and so on. Let the team members decide on the "how it's going to get done" elements. Should they go a bit off

the track, you can always fine-tune. Or, better yet, *lead a discussion* on how they can fine-tune.

- *It's expected.* State clearly, from the outset, that the team members will be expected to develop the answers to work-related issues—it will be *their responsibility.*

- *We know that you know the answers.* You're an alpha personality, a problem solver. You can come up with "the answer" to virtually anything. You've done it countless times. That's great. Congratulations. You've created organizational codependency. So, now, take a new tack: Let your people come up with the solutions. When someone comes to you with a question, ask them: "What's your recommendation?" They *will* find the answer. And why not—you picked great people for your team, right?

- *Tread lightly on the gas pedal:* Initially, you may have to take a more overt role, in terms of direction and support. Once they start "getting it" and build a confidence level, ease off on the throttle. I know it's tough—the knee-jerk reaction is to swoop in and save the day. How do I know? I'm a control freak, just like you probably are. Force yourself: Ease off.

- *Skinner was right.* Positive reinforcement works wonders. It's downright frightening to brave failure and be held accountable. When your team, or a team member, hits a home run, lavish praise is in order. Encourage. Reinforce. It works wonders.

**Training and Coaching**

Effective training and coaching is one of the pillars of success to any sustainable innovation program. These tips will help the process go as smoothly as possible:

- *Share the joy.* As well as the frustrations—communicate what is working and not working.
- *Newbies count.* Ensure that newcomers to the team, as well as new managers, are included in all training/coaching programs. Keep everyone on the same page.
- *Pick the right coaches.* Not everyone has the psychological makeup to be the coach. Knowledge is key, obviously. But the coach needs to be able to motivate, mediate, create camaraderie and a sense of selflessness.
- *The one-on-one touch.* Individual coaching provides the privacy and attention that breeds success. I've found that discussions regarding areas for improvement are received and acted upon much better in a private session, away from peers listening in. This can be especially critical with new employees and/or team members.
- *Basics first.* Make certain project management basics are taught, applied, and retaught.
- *The coach's creed.* The ideal coach has self-discipline, superior skill sets, a wide and deep understanding of the innovation program's goals, and first-tier communication skills, in order to address both group and one-on-one situations. A coach with these skills can quickly develop acolytes that, in time, become coaches themselves. And that is the dream scenario: the coach/leader who ultimately cultivates future leaders.

**Idea Management Process**

Ideation and the management of the ideation process pack the front end of the NPD funnel with a wealth of viable concepts. This portfolio approach anticipates the fact that some concepts will pan out, while others are dropped. My tips on ideation include:

- *Focus, focus, focus.* Remember that depth is better than breadth for quality idea generation. Drill down and maintain focus.
- *Ask the right questions.* This is an art. Questions that are structured properly open new ground for exploration and drive new insights and discoveries. Start with open-ended questions, which keep the initial discussion wide-angle, gradually narrowing to laser precision for focused exploration of new possibilities.
- *Prioritize ideas.* And keep your eye on areas that enhance perceived value, improve customer relations, and capitalize on competitive opportunities.
- *Store best practices.* And be sure to reference them regularly. Remember, also, to create a database of ideation session "discards"—used in combination with other concepts from the group's "toy box," there might be the makings of a winner.
- *Think fast.* Quick idea validation via fast prototyping jump-starts the process. Think in terms of "days" rather than weeks or months.

At this point, let's recap ways to generate these big ideas:

- *Purpose*. The yield of high-quality ideas can be significantly higher with a clear business purpose and a supportive business sponsor.
- *Timeliness*. So often, the difference between a great idea and a so-so concept is market or technology timing. Your competitors are nipping at your heels. Speed it up!
- *Diversity*. The pool of contributors needs to be broad—perhaps broader than you might think. Cross-pollinate, selecting talent from various divisions, operating units, and so on.
- *Change perspectives*. I've found that really powerful ideas come through individuals who are looking at things in a different way. An idea with potential is like a rough-cut diamond, with many facets. Turn ideas over and over, and examine the various facets, rather than fixate on one particular point of view.
- *Collaborative development*. It is up to the innovation champion to build and nurture an environment where people feel free and unthreatened enough to comment without fear of insult or retribution. This culture of collaboration will enhance the overall yield of high-impact ideas.

**Observe and Measure**

Observation and measurement—in terms of the performance of the program implementation needs to be built-in as a recurring element:

- *What's measured is treasured.* And that's just human nature, so be sure to check and recheck performance monthly. No exceptions, no excuses.
- *What to look for?* The key performance indicators and metrics include:
  - ◆ Research-and-development (R&D) spending as a percentage of sales
  - ◆ Total patents filed/pending/awarded/rejected
  - ◆ Total R&D head count
  - ◆ Current-year percentage of sales attributable to new products released in the past year/three years/five years
  - ◆ Number of new products released

**Net Result and Reward**

The fruits of your team's labor benefit all. These successes must be rewarded, and in the appropriate manner:

- *Innovation and return on investment (ROI).* True innovation results in value creation for all stakeholders, in terms of financial return, increased market share, and enhanced profitability; this is the ultimate goal of your sustainable innovation program.
- *The right rewards.* Rewards and recognition systems can take many forms, from a bonus percentage based on new product sales to peer acknowledgment and awards.
- *Financial rewards.* People have more than one motivating force, which is important to understand, in order to achieve optimal performance. Financial rewards are always nice. For some creative folks, recognition may be an even more powerful driver.
- *Recognition.* Pride . . . a thorny problem solved . . . the personal satisfaction of a job well done—these are some of the intrinsic motivators that make creative people tick. Recognition that communicates a team member's accomplishments can be a powerful tool for the savvy innovation champion. These non-financial rewards can:
  - Raise the commitment level of valued employees
  - Enhance morale and motivate future performance
  - Generate organization-wide "good vibes"
  - Reinforce ideal outcomes
  - Create a powerful linkage between strategy and innovation outcomes

## Or If You *Really* Want Your Innovation Program to Flop . . .

Just for fun, let's turn that checklist on its head for a moment. We asked our friend, Jeff Lindsay, PhD, coauthor of *Conquering Innovation Fatigue* (John Wiley & Sons, 2009), what are the Bizarro World rules of innovation—the anti–*Robert's Rules of Innovation*, if you will? Jeff is the director of Solution Development at Innovationedge, a U.S. patent agent, an inventor with more than 100 patents, and the former corporate patent strategist of Kimberly-Clark Corporation.

His areas of specialty: the personal side of innovation and how "innovation fatigue factors" create barriers to success. According to Jeff, you will make sure your sustainable innovation program is a complete flop if you:

- Never prepare for the inevitable decline of optimism when things get rough and never realize that wild optimism can cause an organization fatigue factor.
- Never look for the trouble around the next corner and remain inflexible in terms of your original plan.
- Never conduct due diligence on competitors' patents until you're well down the road to development.
- Don't handle early registration of domain names for the brand, or think about trademarks and related IP issues.
- Never drop the organization's "sacred cows" even when it's clear they won't pan out.
- Champions: Never take your ego out of the equation.
- Minimize time spent to train or coach teams.
- Never bother to develop measurement tools in advance.

- Trivialize the importance of team diversity.
- Fail to allocate sufficient resources—financial, head count, and so on—to the program.
- Don't establish a clearly understood, system-wide NPD process.
- Fail to get C-level buy-in and ownership.
- Ignore the need to have a strategic vision for sustainable innovation.
- Never link the innovation program to an overarching strategy.
- Spend time focusing on quality ideation at the front-end funnel? *Nah.*

## Advice and Encouragement from the Pros: A Roundtable Discussion

With a network of business associates in various industries from around the world, I thought this parting chapter would be a perfect time to share some of their verbatim comments, in a roundtable discussion, Q&A format.

We have with us: Nic Hunt (director of innovation for an international manufacturing corporation), Bruce Sauter (formerly of Atari and Kohler Company), Ralph Howard (Vice President, Specialty Brands, W.W. Grainger), Hannes Hunschofsky (President, Hoerbiger Corporation of America), Fabio Salik (former managing director, Primary Packaging and Prescription, Rexam), Walter Hester (owner and founder, Maui Jim sunglasses), Greg Lins (President and CEO, TLG Innovation Inc.), Dr. Harlan Weisman (Chief Science & Technology Officer, Medical Devices and Diagnostics, Johnson & Johnson), Jill McCurdy (head of Rexam Plastic Packaging's Innovation Center).

Hope you enjoy their delicious candor as much as I did.

**Robert Brands:** What do you see as some of the biggest stumbling blocks to successful programs for sustainable innovation?

**Nic Hunt:** So much depends on the characteristics of the leader. The absolute wrong way to go is with an innovation champion that is all about the "culture of me." It's all me, me, me.

**Bruce Sauter:** It's got to be a holistic approach. All the pieces have to work together, in a culture where quality ideas are valued, respected, and executed—and the organization must be aligned to foster these great ideas. Balanced across functions. With certain basic values to get this passion harnessed.

**Ralph Howard:** Two words: dominant logic. The concept was introduced by C. K. Prahalad and Richard Bettis more than 20 years ago and refers to the prevailing wisdom within you, or within your organization. It's the orientation, or bias.

**RB:** Isn't that like saying "experience is the best teacher"?

**Ralph:** Sure, until it reaches the point where learned behaviors, or dominant logic, are blinding, or restricting. It becomes the easy "default" setting—a crutch or anchor that keeps the company from sailing into more opportunistic—more innovative—waters. That's where you need to live.

**RB:** You have to "live" it—sustainable innovation—every day, isn't that really it?

**Hannes Hunschofsky:** You need that elemental entrepreneurial spirit, in the classic sense, you know: "Let's try it!" There needs to be tolerance for failure, the will to try something new even if it fails (but the discipline to make that particular mistake only once). You need to show, credibly, that you embrace change. Otherwise, it's never going to happen.

**RB:** Do you notice a wide variance in terms of what professionals see as "innovation"?

**Fabio Salik:** This discussion really got me thinking about innovation programs I've been part of over the years, and I would say the definition of innovation can vary. This really triggers a red light in my mind. Some innovations I've been involved with were prompted by customer requirements, for example.

**Walter Hester:** In a competitive business such as ours, product differentiation is the key to success. Each "innovation" doesn't have to be a home run, although we've had our share of those. Little things, incremental improvements, can make a huge difference.

**RB:** What about motivating innovation? I remember, a few years ago, reading how Netflix created a competition to see who could improve its system's precision by 10 percent, and offered a $1 million award.

**Nic:** I go back to what I said earlier: Successful innovation is all about turning ideas into money. There needs to be a clear business strategy, and, within this, the contribution of the innovation to the delivery of the strategy must be quantified.

**Greg Lins:** Sounds good. For what it's worth, my views of critical success factors go back to:

- Engage highly talented people, whether permanent or contract.
- Relentlessly work to increase the capacity of these most innovative and valuable employees.

- Aggressively reduce the costs of performing routine tasks, freeing resources for innovation.
- Develop compensation systems tied to business metrics—outcomes of properly focused innovation, not innovation itself.

**RB:** How does your fourth point work?

**Greg:** I've been involved with some work where we used some alternative metrics that worked very well, such as development of a strategic set of brand promises, and measuring the rate of promises made and promises kept. This is an easy way to boil down all of the business metrics into things that are actionable for most people, which everyone can agree upon.

**RB:** Innovation in a large versus a smaller organization— let's go there for a moment.

**Dr. Harlan Weisman:** My sense is that it's actually easier to institute in the smaller to midsized organization, where innovation really can mean "survival," where your very existence depends on the outcome of the ideation. That fear can really energize the group.

**Jill McCurdy:** Big or small, it's important to tie the ideation piece to the big-picture strategy, and to really "live" the project.

**Nic:** Big company or small, when the strategy is undefined, the end result is undefined—as when it's "we'll know it when we see it." The strat plan is the start. From there, it's project management: the number of projects at each stage, the time it takes to make it through each stage, watching for drifts—"mission creep" is what it's called.

**RB:** Good ideas really matter and require carefully cultivated talent and a "tool box," no?

**Jill:** Once you get into ideation sessions, remember that it's not all about props, scenarios, and "creative play." You don't need an "ideation room." You can do it in a lunchroom, at a customer's conference room. What you *do* need is a group that's alive, living the problem—it's about the people in the room and their connection to the product. That includes the facilitator. And speaking of the people in the room, for ideation sessions, try and select people who aren't too aligned with each other.

**Bruce:** The ideal scenario is where creativity is so part of the culture that ideas flow from production workers, from everyone. The entire organization wants to pitch in and does pitch in. It's step by step, but, with consistency, it does happen.

**Hannes:** Very true. We get hundreds of ideas from within the organization, on paper, in emails. Such a culture is not created over the weekend, though. It takes time and requires a tolerance for failure; we learn from failure.

**Walter:** The emails keep coming in, with ideas. People feel free to contribute.

**Ralph:** At Kohler Company, where I was VP–Sales, we prided ourselves on our position as a designer leader in kitchen and bath fixtures.

**RB:** I remember well how Herb Kohler, grandson of the founder, personally headed every NPD meeting.

**Ralph:** Right, and in that environment we developed the tankless Purist® Hatbox® toilet, such a fresh, minimalist design for Western cultures—and our cultural bias, or dominant logic, regarding what a toilet looks like and how it functions. A success, starting at more than \$4,000! Now that's challenging convention through breakthrough ideation.

**Nic:** Remember that ideation can be used to fill the hopper with potential developments, as well as to resolve roadblocks that require creative solutions. Looking back at the big picture, however, success requires a culture change from the top down. It's complex, it takes time, and it's worth it all—if you're serious about survival.

## Sustainable Innovation and You

I hope that by reading *Robert's Rules of Innovation* you have gained an understanding of the dire need for sustainable innovation, what it takes to set the stage for such a program, the specific requirements and tactics needed, and the encouragement to make this effort a reality in your organization. Apply our 10 imperatives in all facets of your innovation program.

As our roundtable participants say, it's not easy, it isn't done overnight, and it is well worth the effort to do it right.

Remember, as you plan your attack on the innovation status quo, that this effort will require consistency, communications, and collaboration, in order to forge an exciting new culture.

It will take bold leadership and buy-in from the highest levels of the organization. A strategic plan must be developed and sold in, up and down the company. The right people, from diverse disciplines, must be identified, recruited, trained, and motivated. Successes and failures must be communicated, regularly. An innovation process must be created and implemented, and results measured and reported.

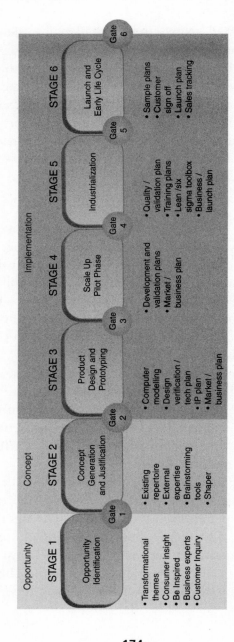

**Exhibit 8.2   Example of New Product Development Process**

And it will be done. It's common knowledge that people resist change. You will find those that are on board and make sure the naysayers get off the bus at the next station stop.

So what happened to Airspray and its pledge to introduce innovations year after year? The company was publicly traded on the Amsterdam Stock Exchange since 1998 and was purchased by Rexam in the summer of 2006 at a premium of 15x EBIT, thanks in great measure to our painstakingly created innovation and patent portfolio. The products were integrated into Rexam's Personal Care Division and they remain the industry's widest and deepest line of foam dispenser.

Because sustainable innovation is your ticket to the future. It's innovate or die—and I have a strong sense which option you'll choose.

Now you know.

# Product Development Process

Exhibits A.1 and A.2 show the new product development (NPD) process at Airspray, makers of the innovative mechanical finger-pump foamers.

# Workflow R&D Project

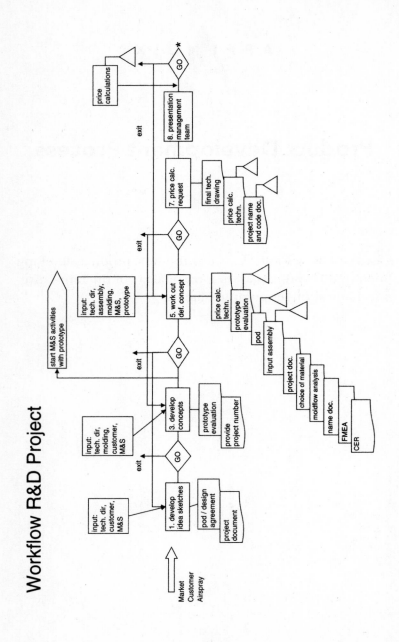

**0 compose project team**
making project directory
making planning R&D
making project document
form a project team

**1 prod. dev.**
work out sketch ideas
program of demands for own project
design agreement for customer project

**2 prod. dev. and tech. dir**
go/no go
Rexam Airspray project: register in project document
customer project: communicate with customer

**3 prod. dev.**
upscale ideas to concepts
question form for prototype
add prototype in prototype registration (Excel)

**4 prod. dev. and tech. dir**
go/no go
Rexam Airspray project: register in project document

**5 prod. dev.**
work out final concept
price calculation drawing
register assemblage demands in project doc
complete evaluation prototype
complete pod/design agreement
customer project: presentation for customer

**6 management**
go/no go
Rexam Airspray project: register in project document
customer project: communicate with customer

**7 molding/logistic manager**
Request for price calculations
price calculation drawings: registration in access (ID)
registration to whom offer is being send (also SW models)
archiving price calculation moulders in docuware
Choose project name/code deliberate with M&S and logistics

**8 project leader**
presentation for management team

**9 management**
go/no go
based on CER
Airspray project: register in project document
customer project: communicate with customer

**Exhibit A.1   PD Process Flow Part I**
*Source:* Norbert De Jong.

179

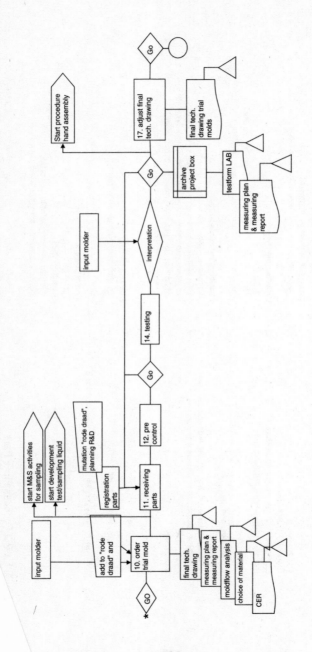

start M&S activities for sampling

start development test/sampling liquid

mutation "rode draad", planning R&D

input molder

add to "rode draad" and

registration parts

10. order trial mold

11. receiving parts

12. pre control

14. testing

input molder

interpretation

GO

Go

Go

Go

final tech. drawing

measuring plan & measuring report

moldflow analysis

choice of material

CER

archive project box

testform LAB

measuring plan & measuring report

17. adjust final tech. drawing

final tech. drawing trial molds

Start procedure hand assembly

**10 molding dev.**
order trial molds through access
tech. drawing registration in access (with ID)
sending tech. drawing / SW-files documented in access
planning new molds documented in "rode draad" and planning R&D
making measure plan and measuring report for R&D (prod.dev.)
analyze parts in moldflow

**11 molding dev.**
receiving parts
registration parts in access

**12 molding dev.**
Pre-control. Check with report molder

**13 molding dev.**
go/no go, document in measuring report

**14 prod. dev.**
testing/measuring parts
registration of tests in project directory

**15 project team**
interpretation results
documenting conclusions and actions in measure report
communication with molder in docuware.

**16 project team**
go/no go, register in measure report
last run from trial mold save as reference parts
1 shot of all trial molds save in document box

**17 prod. dev.**
adjusting final tech. drawing

**18 management**
go/no go
go for next phase of the project
documenting in project document

note: order trial/production molds depending
of the situation it can happen that first a trial mold is made and then a production mold
But it also can happen that only a production or a trial mold is made

**Legend**

start/ trigger
process
decision
input
connection

document
completed document
connector to next process
internal storage

**Exhibit A.1** *(continued)*

181

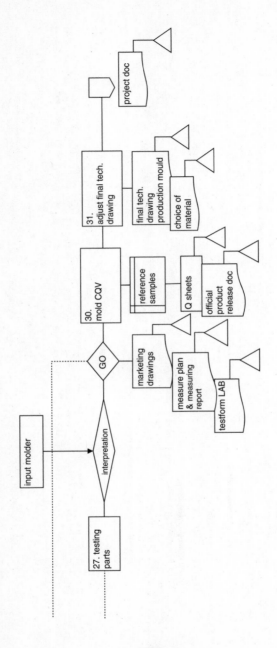

**27 prod. dev.**
testing/measuring parts
testing documented in project dir.
conclusion in test report or measure report

**28 project team**
interpretation
conclusions and actions documented in measure report

**29 project team**
go/no go
when no go tech. drawings will be adapted
feedback on changes to assembly, QC and the measuring department
all changes documented in measuring report
finalize marketing drawings (prod. dev.) and place them on the web (TSS)

**30 project team**
see separate document Mold CQV
reference samples added to project box
reference samples (as starting point for production)
official/temporary launch decision with project team,
QC, production, assembly and molding
official product launch communicate with total company

**31 prod. dev.**
adapt final tech. drawing

**32 project leader**
finish project
complete project document
samples of all parts in project box
hand over project to molding department

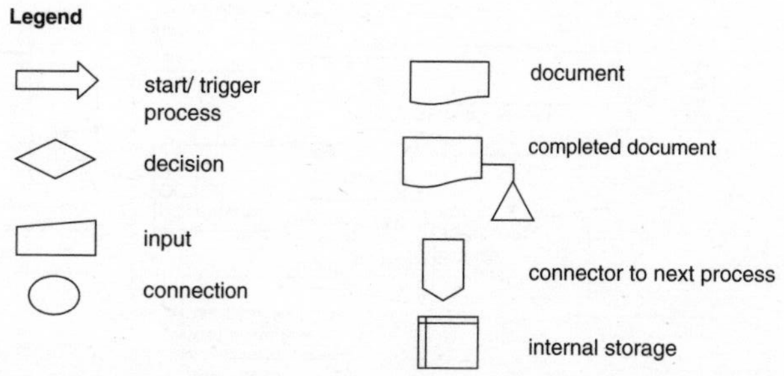

**Legend**

start/ trigger process

decision

input

connection

document

completed document

connector to next process

internal storage

**Exhibit A.2  PD Process Flow Part II**

183

# Workflow R&D Project

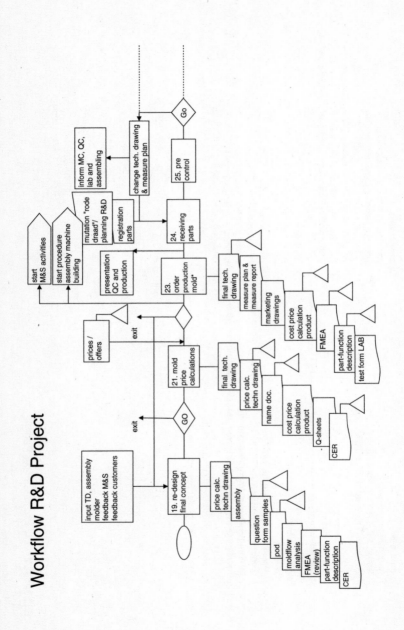

**19 prod. dev.**
redesign final concept
input documented in project document
design sketches and ideas in project map (computer and paper)

**20 tech. dir.**
go/no go
Airspray project: register in project document
customer project: communicate with customer

**21 molding developm./logistic man**
request for price calculations
offer drawing registration in access (ID)
registration to whom offer is being sent (also SW models)
archiving offer drawing
archiving price calculation molders in docuware
document name and codes

**22 management Rexam ASI and/or RDS**
go/no go
based on CER
Airspray project: register in project document
customer project: communicate with customer

**23 molding**
ordering product molds, documenting in access
tech. drawing in access with ID
sending tech. drawing / SW-files documente in access
planning new molds documented in "rode draad" and planning R&D
making measure plan and measuring report for R&D (prod.dev.)
present new product for QC and production

**24 molding dev.**
receiving parts
registration parts in access

**25 molding dev.**
pre-control, check with report molder

**26 molding dev.**
go/no go
documenting in measuring report

**Exhibit A.2** *(continued)*

185

A Focus on the Process of Product Development and Launch

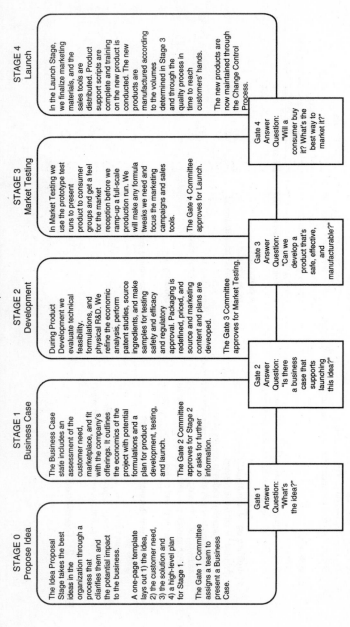

**STAGE 0**
**Propose Idea**

The Idea Proposal Stage takes the best ideas in the organization through a process that clarifies them and the potential impact to the business.

A one-page template lays out 1) the idea, 2) the customer need, 3) the solution and 4) a high-level plan for Stage 1.

The Gate 1 Committee assigns a team to present a Business Case.

**Gate 1**
Answer Question: "What's the idea?"

**STAGE 1**
**Business Case**

The Business Case state includes an assessment of the customer need, marketplace, and fit with the company's offerings. It outlines the economics of the project with potential formulations and a plan for product development, testing, and launch.

The Gate 2 Committee approves for Stage 2 or asks for further information.

**Gate 2**
Answer Question: "Is there a business case that supports launching this idea?"

**STAGE 2**
**Development**

During Product Development we evaluate technical feasibility, formulations, and physical R&D. We refine the economic analysis, perform patent studies, source ingredients, and make samples for testing safety and efficacy and regulatory approval. Packaging is redefined, priced, and source and marketing content and plans are developed.

The Gate 3 Committee approves for Market Testing.

**Gate 3**
Answer Question: "Can we develop a product that's safe, effective, and manufacturable?"

**STAGE 3**
**Market Testing**

In Market Testing we use the prototype test runs to present product to consumer groups and get a feel for the market reception before we ramp-up a full-scale production run. We will make any formula tweaks we need and focus the marketing campaigns and sales tools.

The Gate 4 Committee approves for Launch.

**Gate 4**
Answer Question: "Will a consumer buy it? What's the best way to market it?"

**STAGE 4**
**Launch**

In the Launch Stage, we finalize marketing materials, and the sales tools are distributed. Product support scripts are complete and training on the new product is conducted. The new products are manufactured according to the volumes determined in Stage 3 and through the quality process in time to reach customers' hands.

The new products are now maintained through the Change Control Process.

**Exhibit A.3  Product Development Process Flow**
*Source:* Robert U. Craven.

# APPENDIX B

# The Five Stages of the Production Development Process: Example 1

Exhibits B.1 through B.5 show a five-stage flowchart for product development.

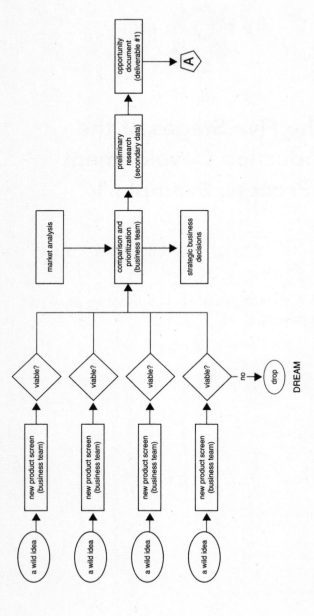

**Exhibit B.1** Dream: A "wild idea" is screened by the business team, judged for viability and, if judged "yes," submitted for comparison and prioritization, with inputs regarding market analytics and strategic business direction. (It is dropped if the judgment is "no go.") The dream then proceeds for preliminary research (secondary data) and on to creation of an "opportunity document"

*Source:* Jeff DeFazio.

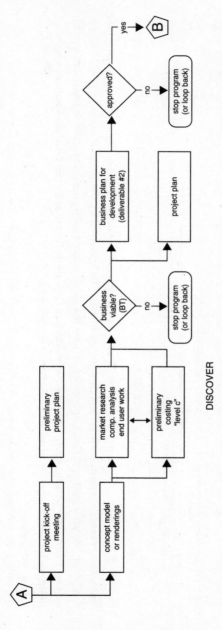

DISCOVER

**Exhibit B.2   Discover:** Next is the project kickoff meeting and concept model. A preliminary project plan is created, market research and a competitive analysis undertaken, and preliminary costing estimated before heading to a viability analysis (go/no go). If yes, the business development plan is created, along with a project plan; then another approval stage. If it's still a go, we head to …

*Source:* Jeff DeFazio.

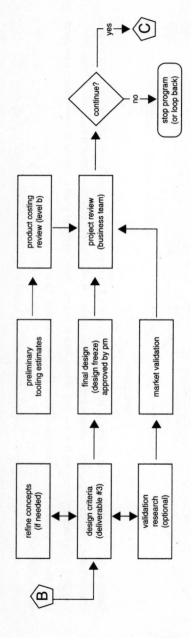

DESIGN

**Exhibit B.3 Design:** Concepts are refined, as necessary, and a design criteria document prepared (and validation research undertaken). A final design is submitted for approval by the product manager. (*IP Alert:* At this point, file your patents!) Once approved, it joins the preliminary tooling estimates (which are submitted for a Level B product costing review) and market validation for a project review by the business team, at which point we hit another go/no-go milestone. And, if it's still a go ...

*Source:* Jeff DeFazio.

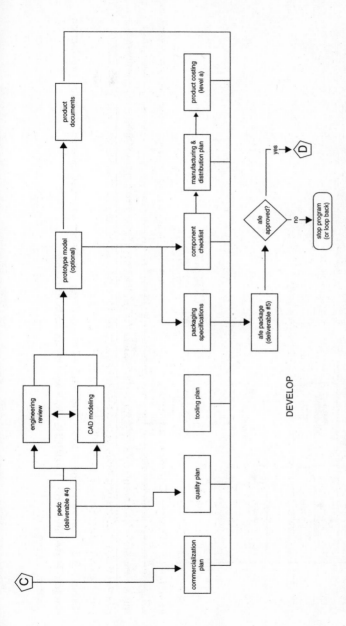

**Exhibit B.4 Develop:** A variety of plans are created (commercialization, quality, tooling, packaging, components, manufacturing and distribution, costing) along with CAD modeling, prototyping, and product documentation—and synthesized into another review package, where the next go/no-go milestone occurs. Here, we either loop back for refinements or proceed to Stage 5 . . .

*Source:* Jeff DeFazio.

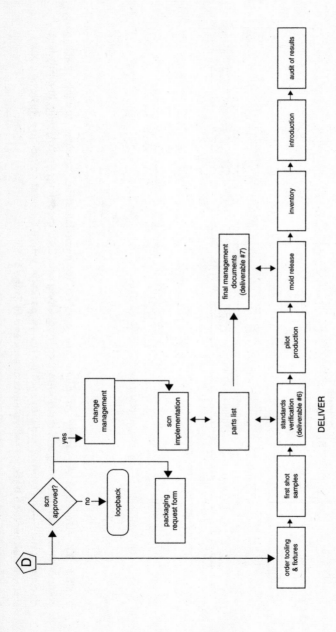

**Exhibit B.5** Deliver: Where tools and fixtures are ordered, first shot samples created, to pilot production, mold release, inventory, LAUNCH!—followed by an audit of results.

*Source:* Jeff DeFazio.

# APPENDIX C

# The Five Stages of the Production Development Process: Example 2

Appendix C shows the "Idea Hopper" and the details of a five-stage product development process.

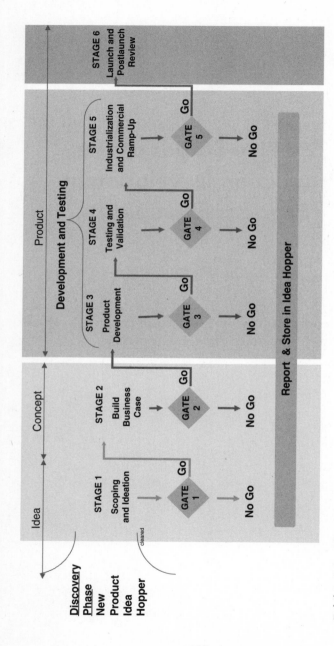

Exhibit C.1  Idea Hopper

194

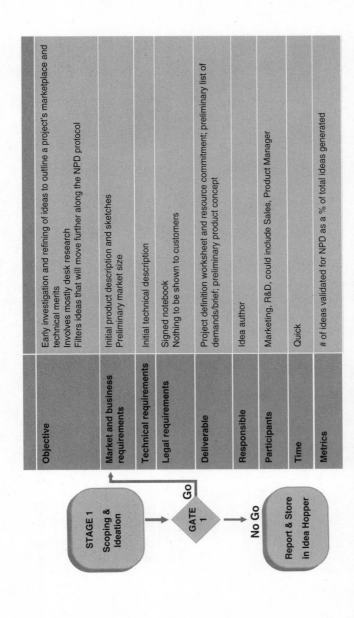

| | |
|---|---|
| Objective | Early investigation and refining of ideas to outline a project's marketplace and technical merits<br>Involves mostly desk research<br>Filters ideas that will move further along the NPD protocol |
| Market and business requirements | Initial product description and sketches<br>Preliminary market size |
| Technical requirements | Initial technical description |
| Legal requirements | Signed notebook<br>Nothing to be shown to customers |
| Deliverable | Project definition worksheet and resource commitment; preliminary list of demands/brief; preliminary product concept |
| Responsible | Idea author |
| Participants | Marketing, R&D, could include Sales, Product Manager |
| Time | Quick |
| Metrics | # of ideas validated for NPD as a % of total ideas generated |

**STAGE 1**
**Scoping & Ideation**

**GATE 1**

**Go**

**No Go**

**Report & Store in Idea Hopper**

Exhibit C.2   Stage 1: Scoping and Ideation

| | |
|---|---|
| **Objective** | Prepare a defined product description, business justification, and detailed plan of action. |
| **Customer involvement** | Market input |
| **Supplier involvement** | Decisions on materials |
| **Market and business requirements** | Strategic fit assessment and portfolio analysis<br>Market analysis; primary/secondary research<br>Consumer target market understanding<br>Target customers analysis and value proposition (benefit to customer)<br>Competitive benchmarking<br>Sales volume objectives and target price |
| **Technical requirements** | Detailed technical assessment.<br>Product features, attributes, performance requirements and specifications, (regulatory reqs.), engineering drawings<br>Performance targets, material trials |
| **Financial requirements** | Cost estimates<br>Revenue and profitability evaluation<br>Financial justification for prototyping |
| **Legal requirements** | Sign confidentiality agreement with customers and suppliers<br>Substantive patent examinations<br>Check for patent infringement on models<br>Identify geographical markets desired<br>File patents |
| **Deliverable** | Preliminary marketing plan<br>Business case (corp approval) for prototype tooling investment |
| **Responsible** | Program Manager, Product Manager |
| **Participants** | Marketing, R&D, Sales, Manufacturing, Finance |
| **Time** | 1 month |
| **Metrics** | # of projects selected to move to Stage 3; # of customer RFQs received and awarded |

**Exhibit C.3  Stage 2: Build Business Case**

196

| | |
|---|---|
| **Objective** | Actual design refinement and physical development of the product tested to ensure the product meets requirements under controlled conditions. Produce low volume samples. |
| **Customer involvement** | Detailed market evaluation Prototype partially tested with customer |
| **Supplier involvement** | Materials |
| **Market and business requirements** | Portfolio strategy development Assess volumes and pricing strategy Completed competitive benchmarking Launch material data gathering plan Initial consumer testing Decide manufacturing location |
| **Technical requirements** | Lab tests, early use tests (regulations) Review performance requirements and product specifications Design for manufacture and automation Define design validation Equipment design and process specification and construction |
| **Financial requirements** | Revenue and profitability evaluation Financial justification for scale-up tooling/moulds |
| **Legal requirements** | Modify/amend/complete patent application up to 1 year. Post initial filing, possibility to apply for a second patent. Freedom to operate around product |
| **Deliverable** | Design validation and validation plan Prototype product, (Possibly: design freeze for clinical trials) Preliminary marketing launch plan Corp Approval Doc for pilot moulds and industrial tooling |
| **Responsible** | Program Manager and Marketing |
| **Participants** | Manufacturing, Sales, R&D, QA, Finance |
| **Time** | Depending on product line complexity: 3–24 months |
| **Metrics** | # of projects selected to move to Stage 4 |

Exhibit C.4   Stage 3: Product Development

| | |
|---|---|
| Objective | Product testing to ensure compliance to customer/consumer needs.<br>Establish production process & conditions via trial or limited production scale runs |
| Customer involvement | Samples tested with customer/customer<br>Customer acceptance (and possibly commitment) |
| Supplier involvement | Raw material and other contracts |
| Market and business requirements | Consumer testing and acceptance trials<br>Rollout and launch strategy<br>Communication plan<br>Sales distribution strategy<br>Sales training plan |
| Technical requirements | Product performance on industrial machines<br>Adjustments for production scale<br>Quality parameters, performance qualifications<br>Final design validation plan<br>Fulfilment and operation strategy |
| Financial requirements | Adjustments to revenue and profitability evaluation<br>Financial justification for industrialization/ for launch |
| Legal requirements | Modify/amend/complete patent application up to 1 year<br>Possibility to apply for multiple patents<br>Freedom to operate around product |
| Deliverable | Final launch plan, data sheets and promotional materials<br>Samples<br>Performance reports<br>Final design freeze<br>Corp approvals for production/industrial tooling |
| Responsible | Program Manager |
| Participants | R&D, Marketing, Sales, Manufacturing, QA |
| Time | Generally 3 months–1.5 years |
| Metrics | # of projects selected to move to Stage 5 |

Exhibit C.5   Stage 4: Testing and Validation

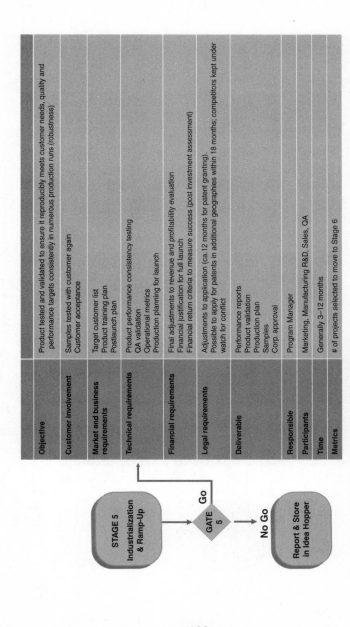

| | |
|---|---|
| Objective | Product tested and validated to ensure it reproducibly meets customer needs, quality and performance targets consistently in numerous production runs (robustness) |
| Customer involvement | Samples tested with customer again<br>Customer acceptance |
| Market and business requirements | Target customer list<br>Product training plan<br>Postlaunch plan |
| Technical requirements | Product performance consistency testing<br>QA validation<br>Operational metrics<br>Production planning for launch |
| Financial requirements | Final adjustments to revenue and profitability evaluation<br>Financial justification for full launch<br>Financial return criteria to measure success (post investment assessment) |
| Legal requirements | Adjustments to application (ca. 12 months for patent granting).<br>Possible to apply for patents in additional geographies within 18 months; competitors kept under watch for conflict |
| Deliverable | Performance reports<br>Product validation<br>Production plan<br>Samples<br>Corp. approval |
| Responsible | Program Manager |
| Participants | Marketing, Manufacturing R&D, Sales, QA |
| Time | Generally 3–12 months |
| Metrics | # of projects selected to move to Stage 6 |

Exhibit C.6   Stage 5: Industrialization and Ramp-Up

| STAGE 6 Launch and Post Launch Review | |
|---|---|
| Objective | Full production and commercial launch and active selling |
| Customer involvement | Multiple customers |
| Market and business requirements | Sales analysis New product flagging<br>PR and awareness campaign<br>Customer roll out tracker<br>Market acceptance data<br>New business development program |
| Technical requirements | Continuous improvements program<br>Supply Chain Management |
| Financial requirements | Measure success<br>Evaluation against forecast and budget |
| Legal requirements | Patent registration granted once patent pending time elapsed<br>Competitors kept under watch for infringement |
| Deliverable | PIA—incl. volume analysis on target product performance, target market, synergy opps., key learning points and audit all output docs<br>Sales reports<br>User market acceptance end-report<br>Quality and cost report |
| Responsible | Program Manager |
| Participants | Sales, Marketing, R&D, Manufacturing |
| Time | Varies by division—TBC |
| Metrics | New products as a % of total sales (will be variable)<br># of patents registered |

Exhibit C.7  Stage 6: Launch and Postlaunch Review

# Key Resources and Links

Within these pages, I've referenced a number of companies and services that specialize in helping companies build robust, sustainable cultures of innovation. For your convenience, I've listed them here.

**www.RobertsRulesofInnovation.com**

- By Innovation Imperative
  - Definition
  - Blog—Updates and additions
  - Tips
  - Video clips

**www.InnovationCoach.com**

- Innovation Resources
  - Innovation Books by Imperative
  - Book Summaries
  - Articles
  - Surveys
  - Tools
  - Video

- Innovation Audit
  - Short
  - In-Depth

## Legal and Patent Resources

www.hoffmannbaron.com

www.barnesrichardson.com

www.fggbb.com

www.uspto.gov

www.patents.com

www.google.com/patents

www.copyright.gov

## Other

www.stage-gate.com

www.vistage.com

www.commstratpr.com

# Acknowledgments

The idea to share my innovation life learnings came in a discussion with my longtime supporter and friend Marty Kleinman, whom I have known for over 15 years and who helped us with public relations. I want to thank him first and foremost for the support and shared enthusiasm in all our endeavors over the years. Without him and his abilities, there would have been no book. A sincere and appreciated *thank you.*

I also want to acknowledge my friends and coworkers (especially at Airspray), mentors, fellow Vistage members, and leaders that helped and inspired me over the years to help me develop into what I have become. Without those who had confidence in me and empowered me to do what had to be done, the success stories would not have followed.

Thank you to my editor, Susan McDermott, at Wiley for believing and supporting the concept. Thank you to Blue Interactive Agency in Ft. Lauderdale and Maria Foes for providing graphic design and exhibits.

And, last but not least, thank you to my wife Janice for her support. With her home backing, our dreams are a lot easier to realize.

—Robert Brands

# About the Authors

**Robert F. Brands** is president and founder of Brands & Company, LLC, and www.innovationcoach.com.

Brands's hands-on experience in bringing innovation to market spans decades, and includes the creation and improvement of product development processes and company culture. He has delivered on his pledge to bring "at least one new product per year to market"—resulting in double-digit profitable growth and shareholder value.

He has led worldwide teams responsible for marketing and sales, operations, and research and development, and is a regular contributor to real- and virtual-world media and social networking platforms.

A native of the Netherlands, Brands earned a bachelor of science in business administration from HTS Eindhoven. A Vistage Member, Member of Tulane University's President's Parent Council, and board member of The Netherlands American Community Trust, Brands is an avid open water diver and a licensed pilot of single-engine aircraft. He resides in Coral Springs, Florida, with his wife and children.

For more information, visit www.linkedin.com/in/robertfbrands.

**Martin Kleinman** is a New York–based business writer and communications specialist (visit www.commstratpr. com). Martin holds a BA degree in economics and psychology from City University of New York at Lehman College. Martin, who enjoys tennis and cycling, resides in Brooklyn with his wife and son. For more information, visit www .linkedin.com/pub/martinkleinman/1/672/16a.

# Index